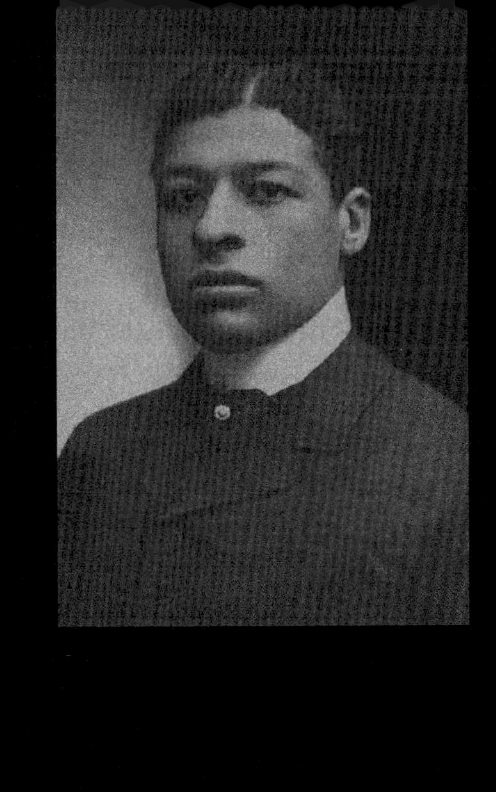

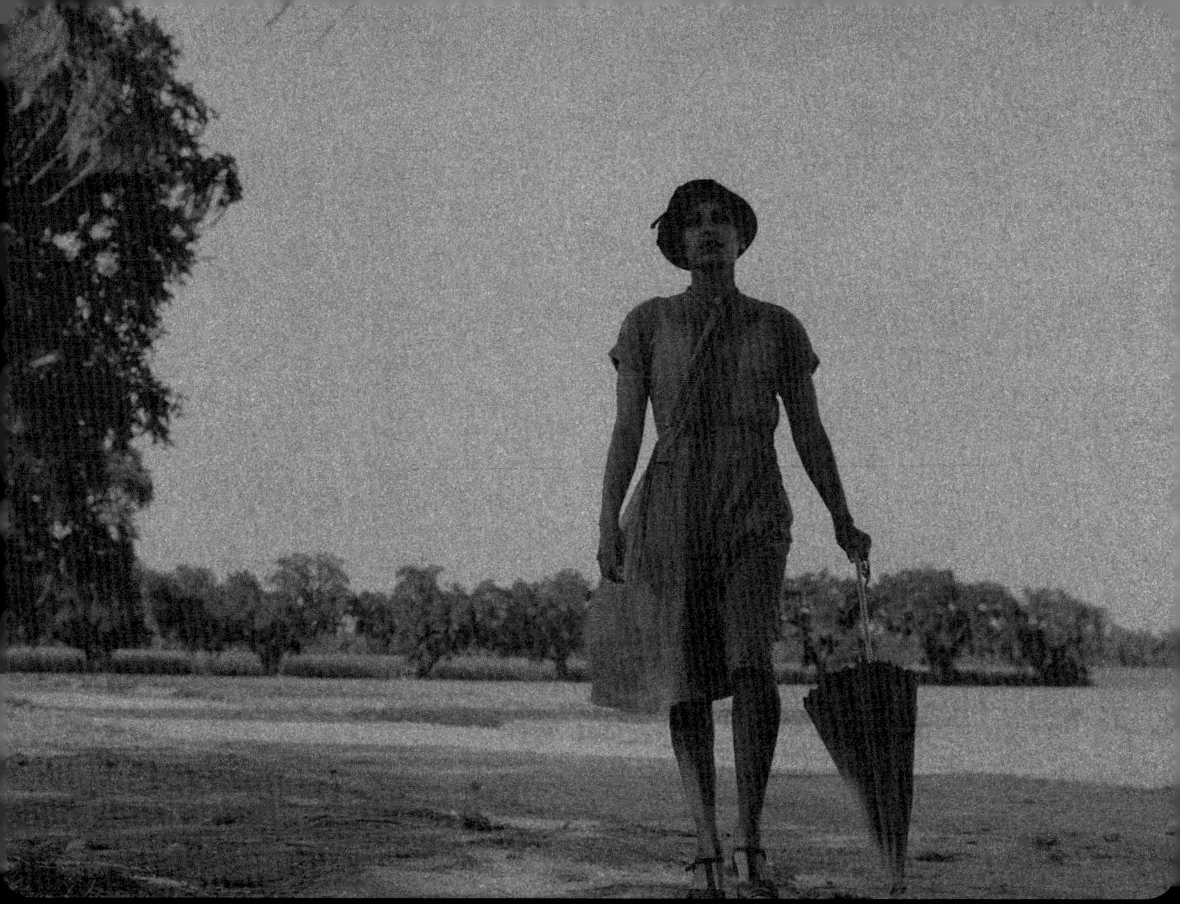

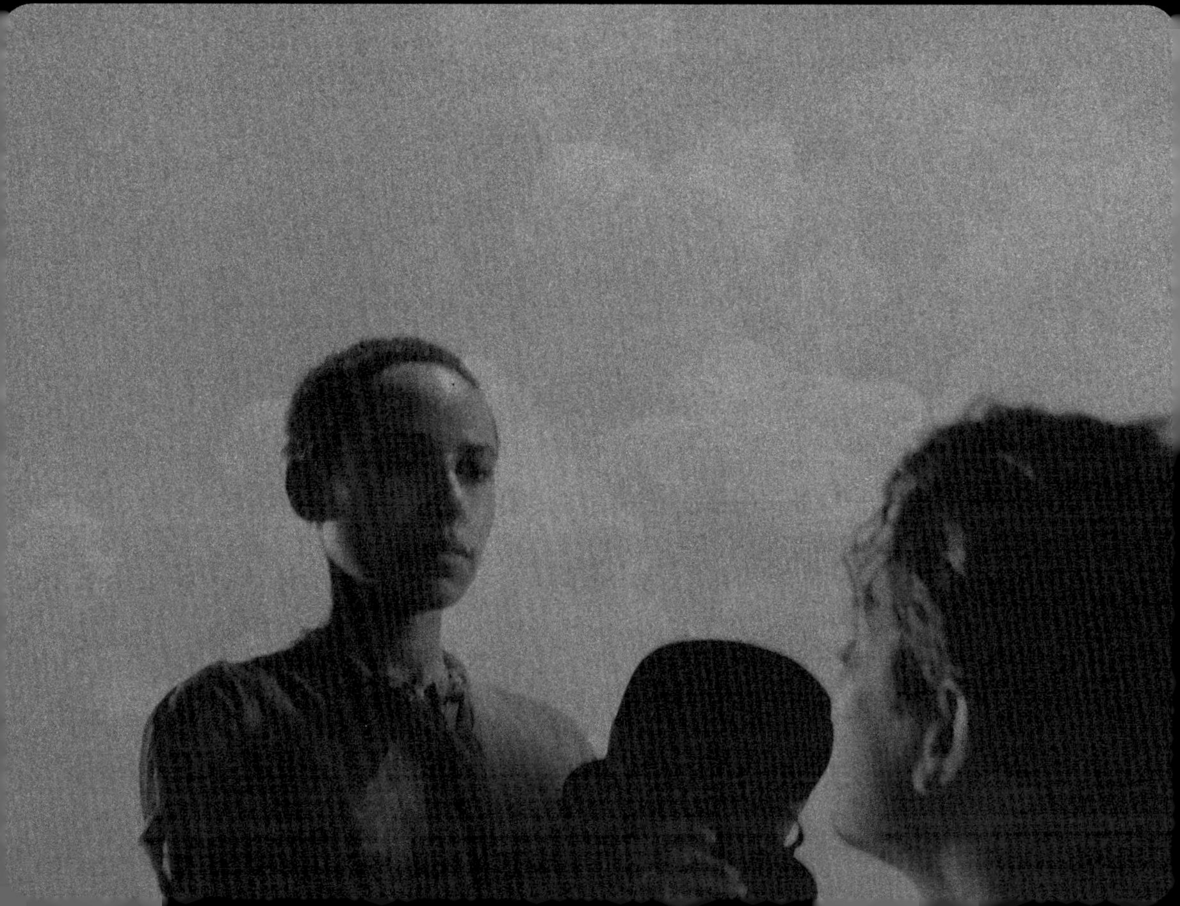

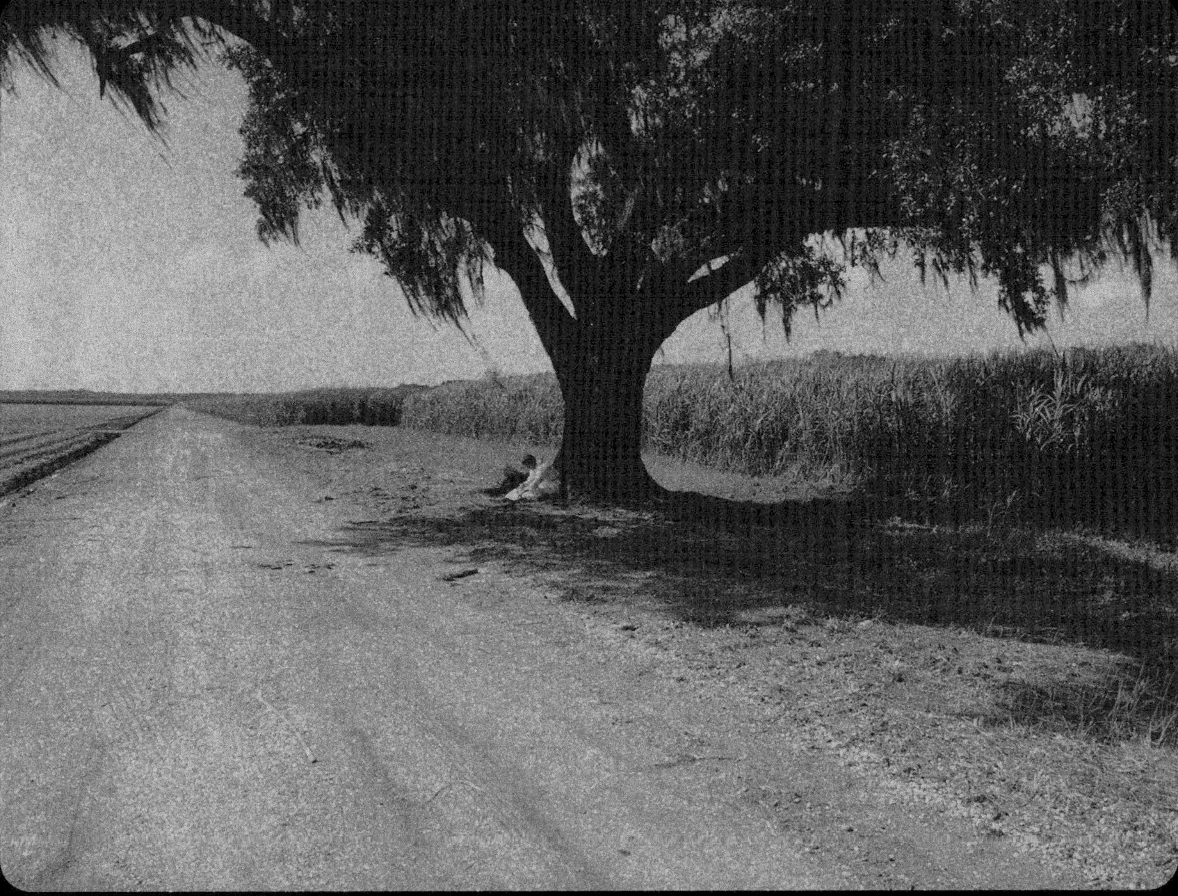

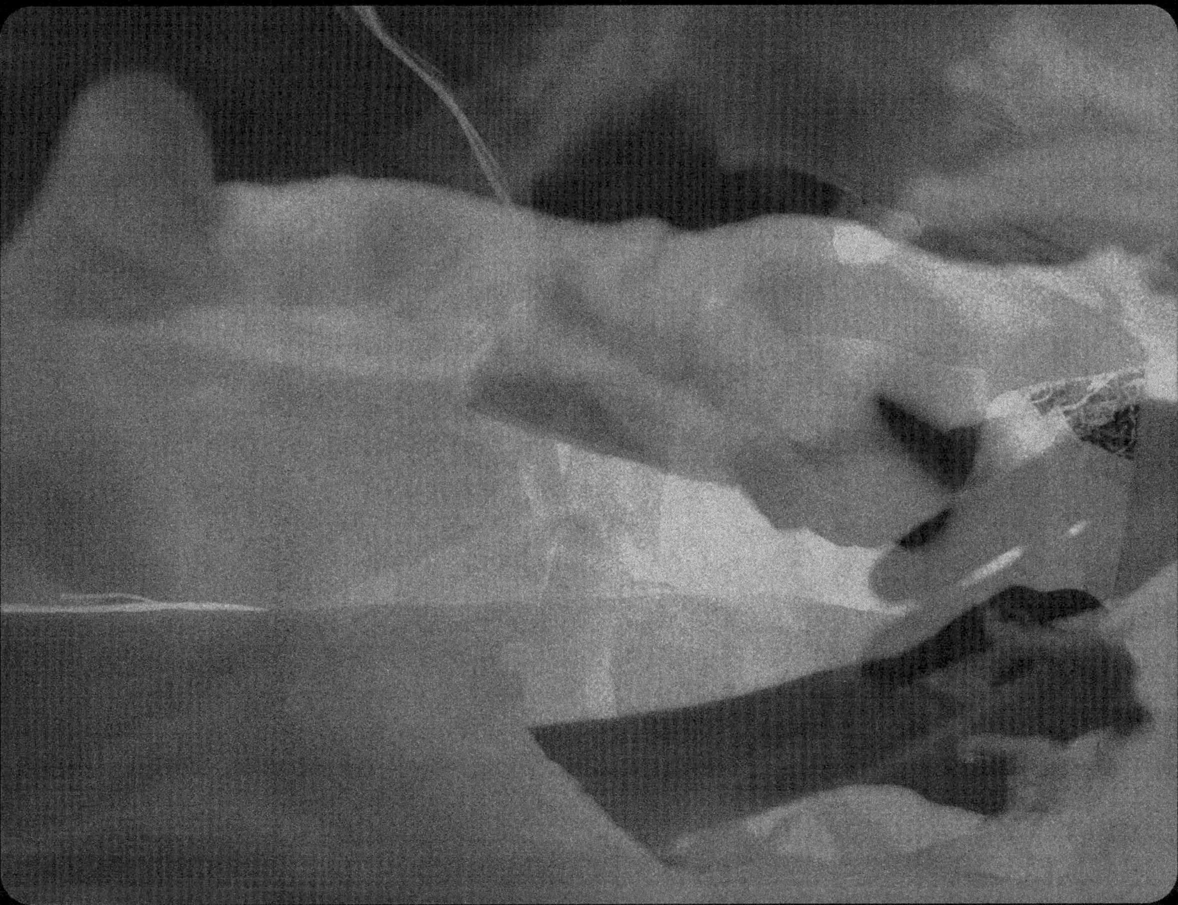

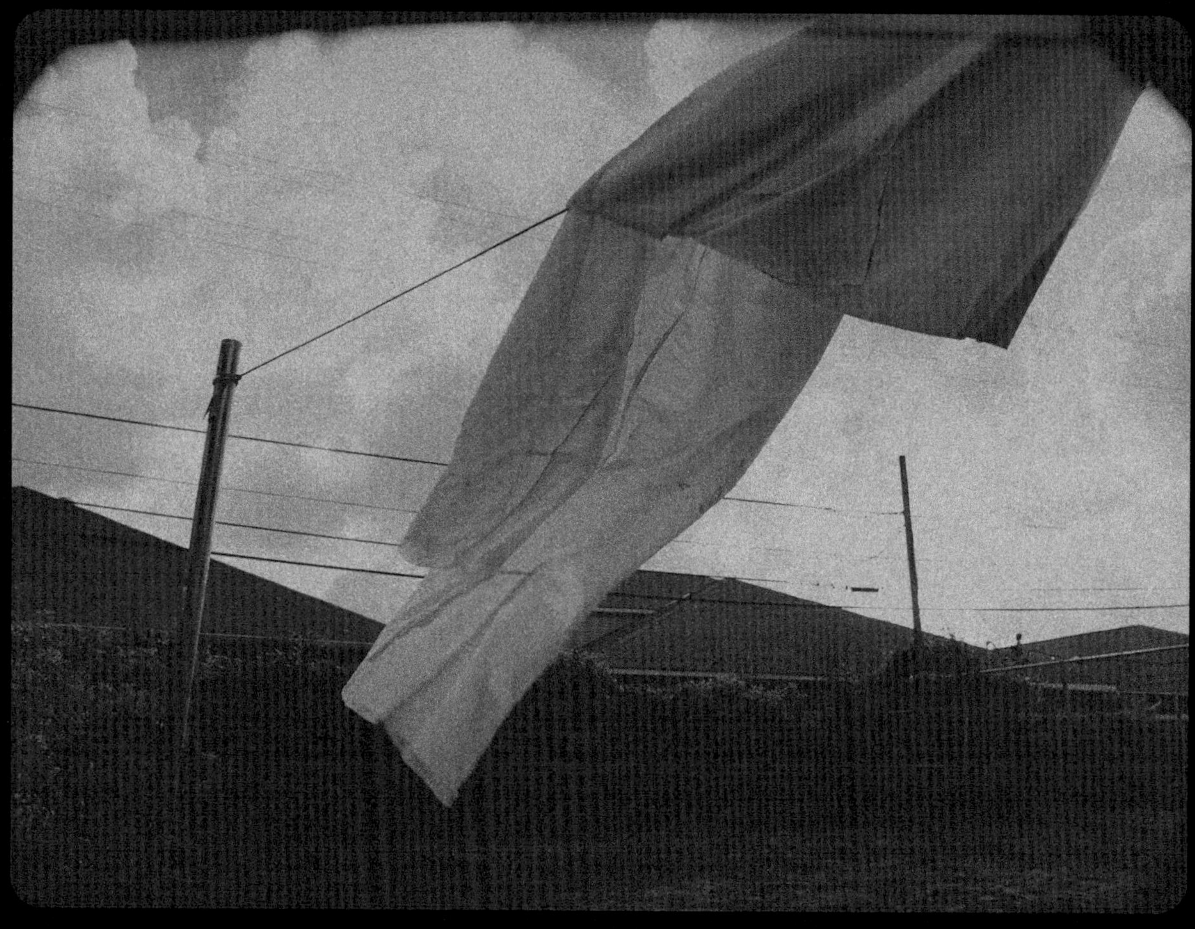

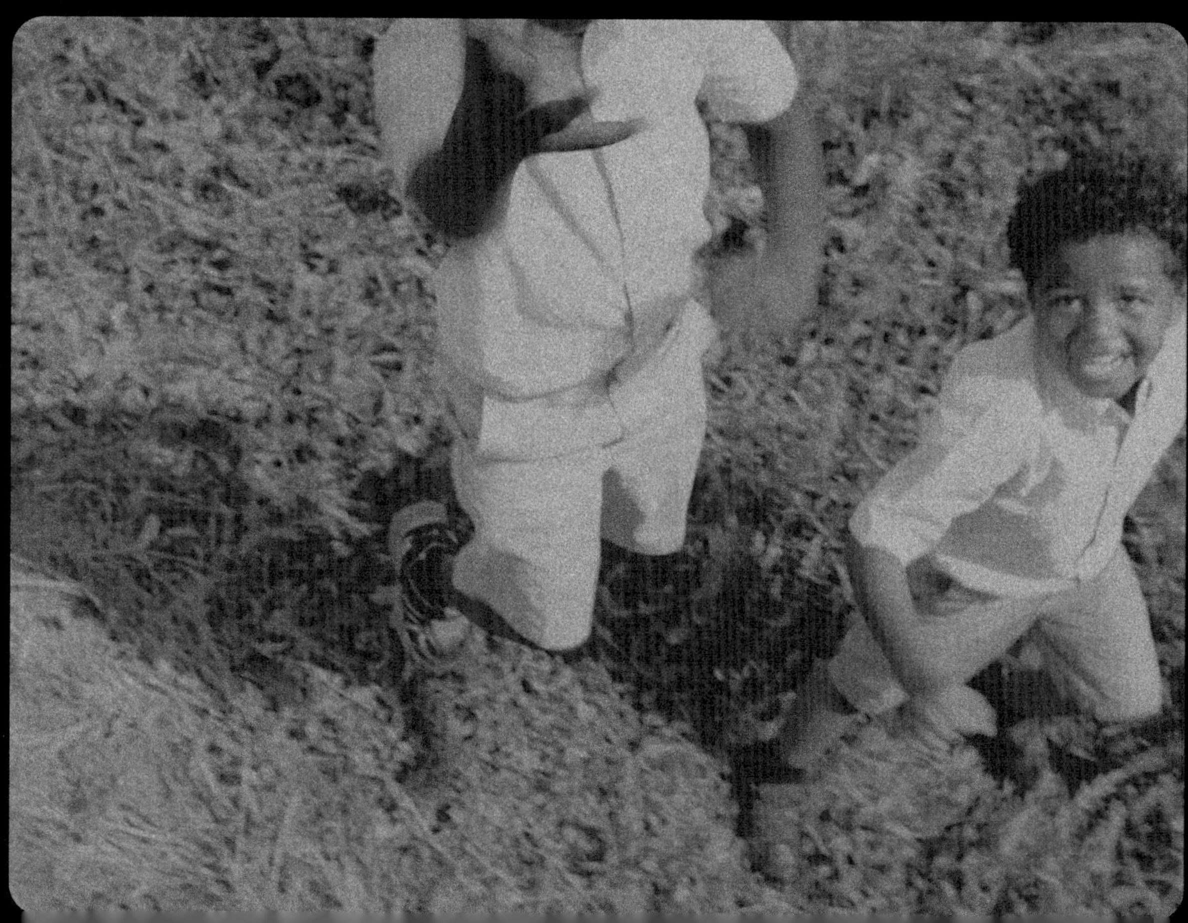

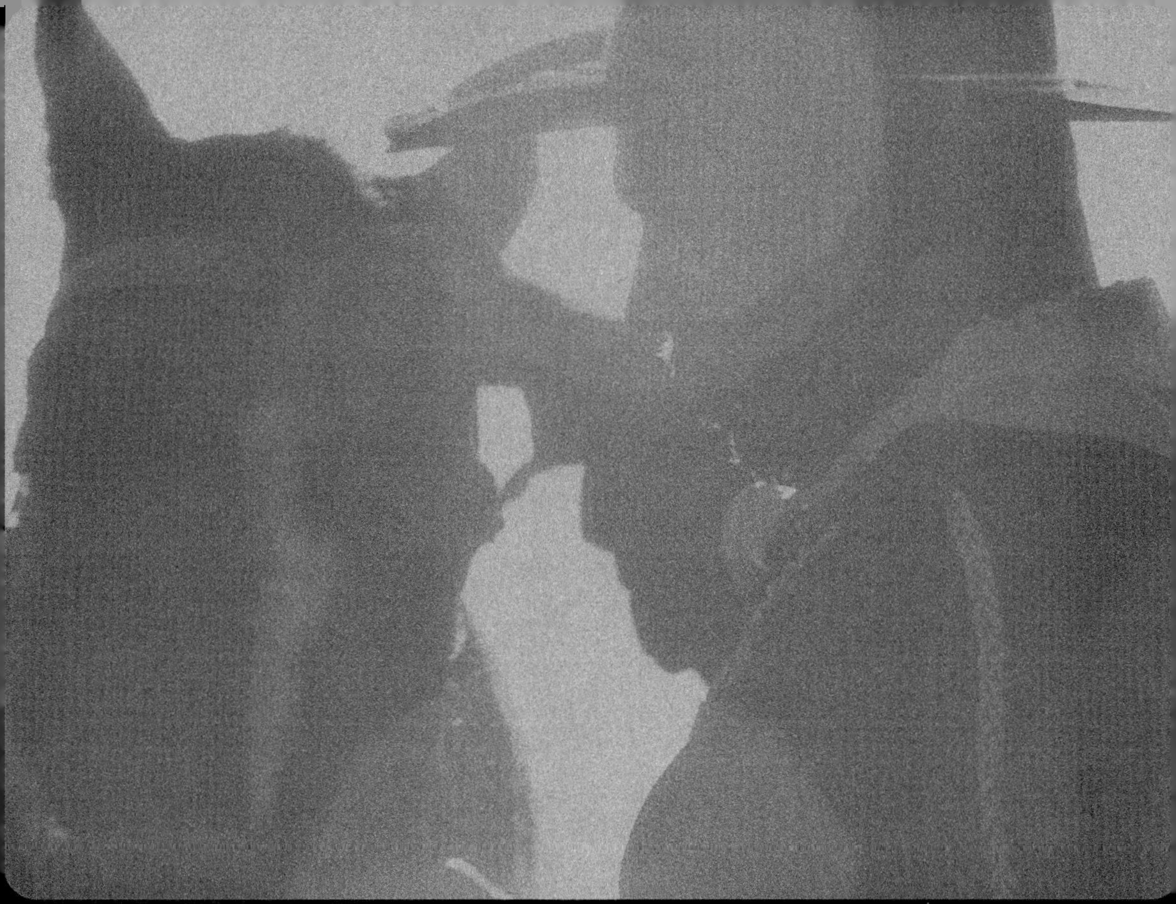

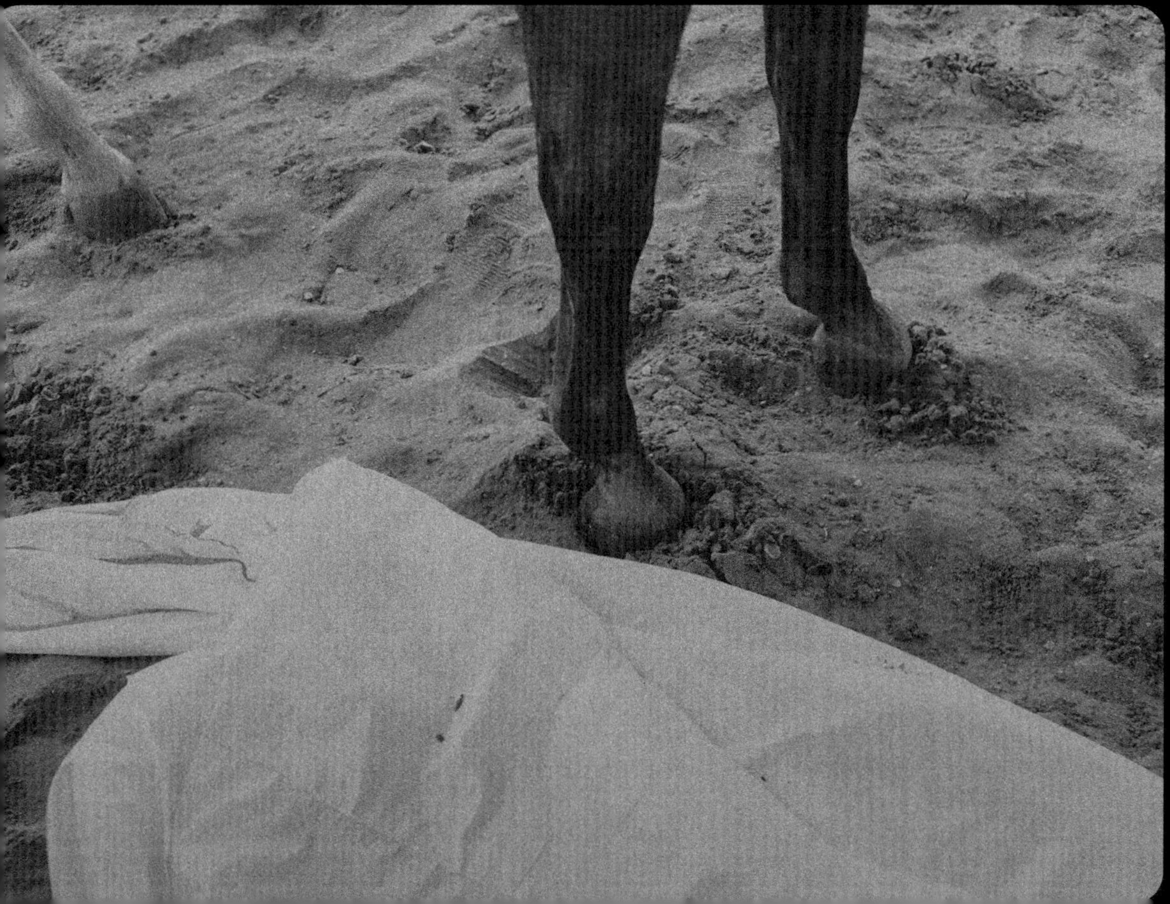

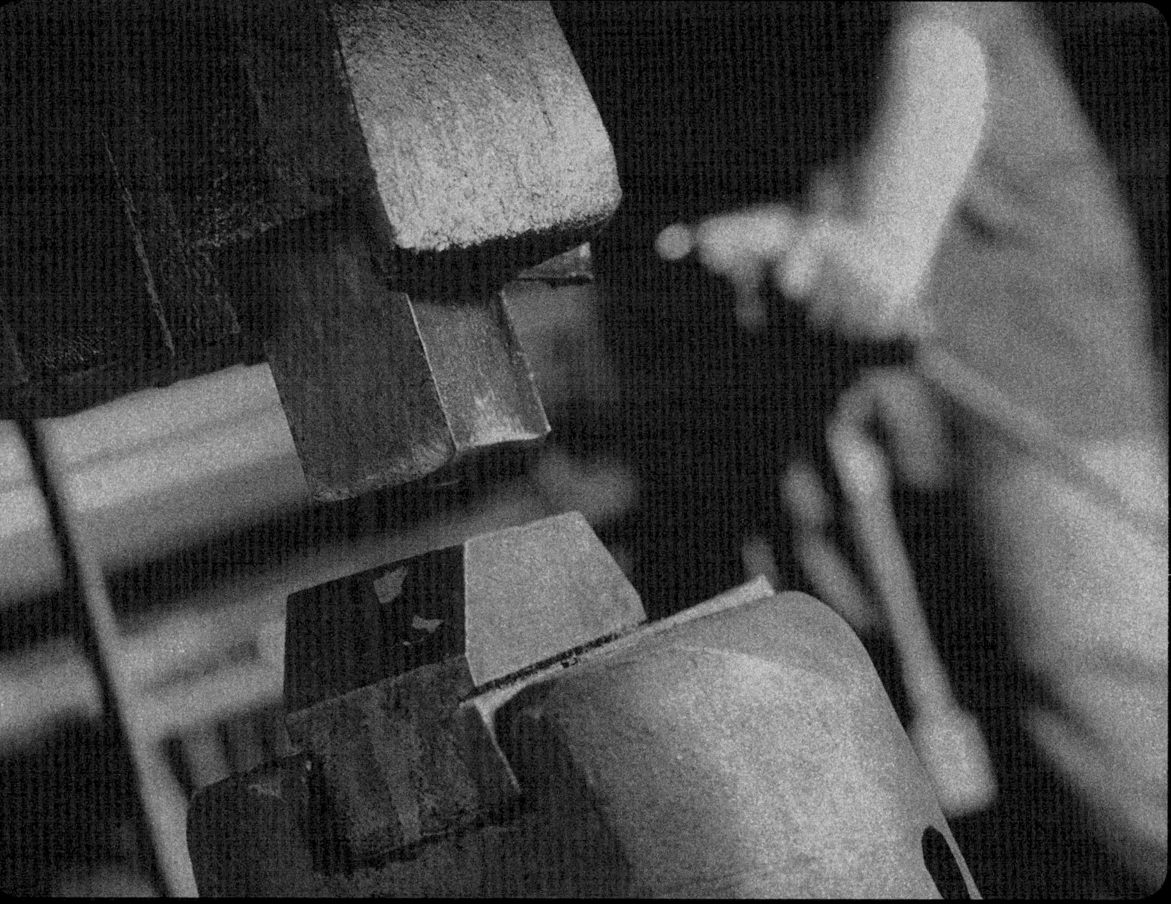

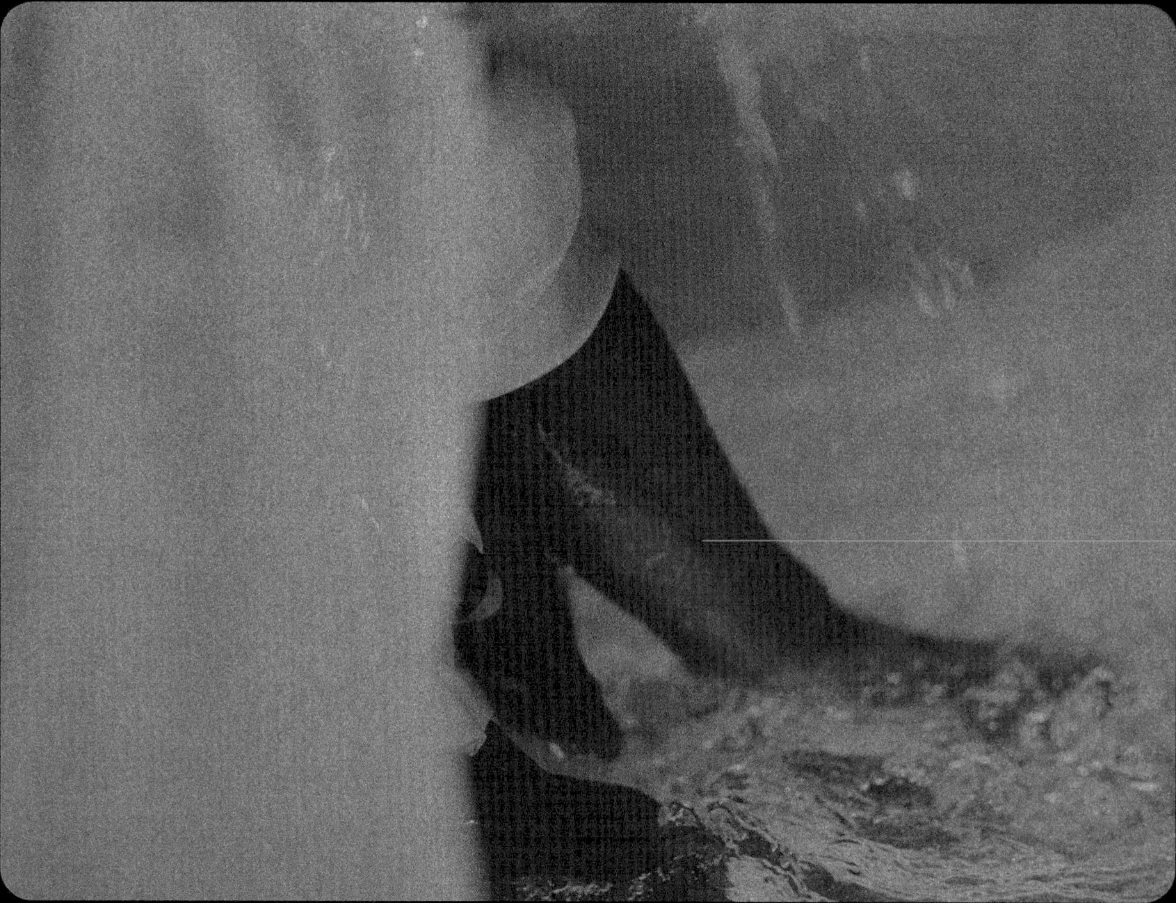

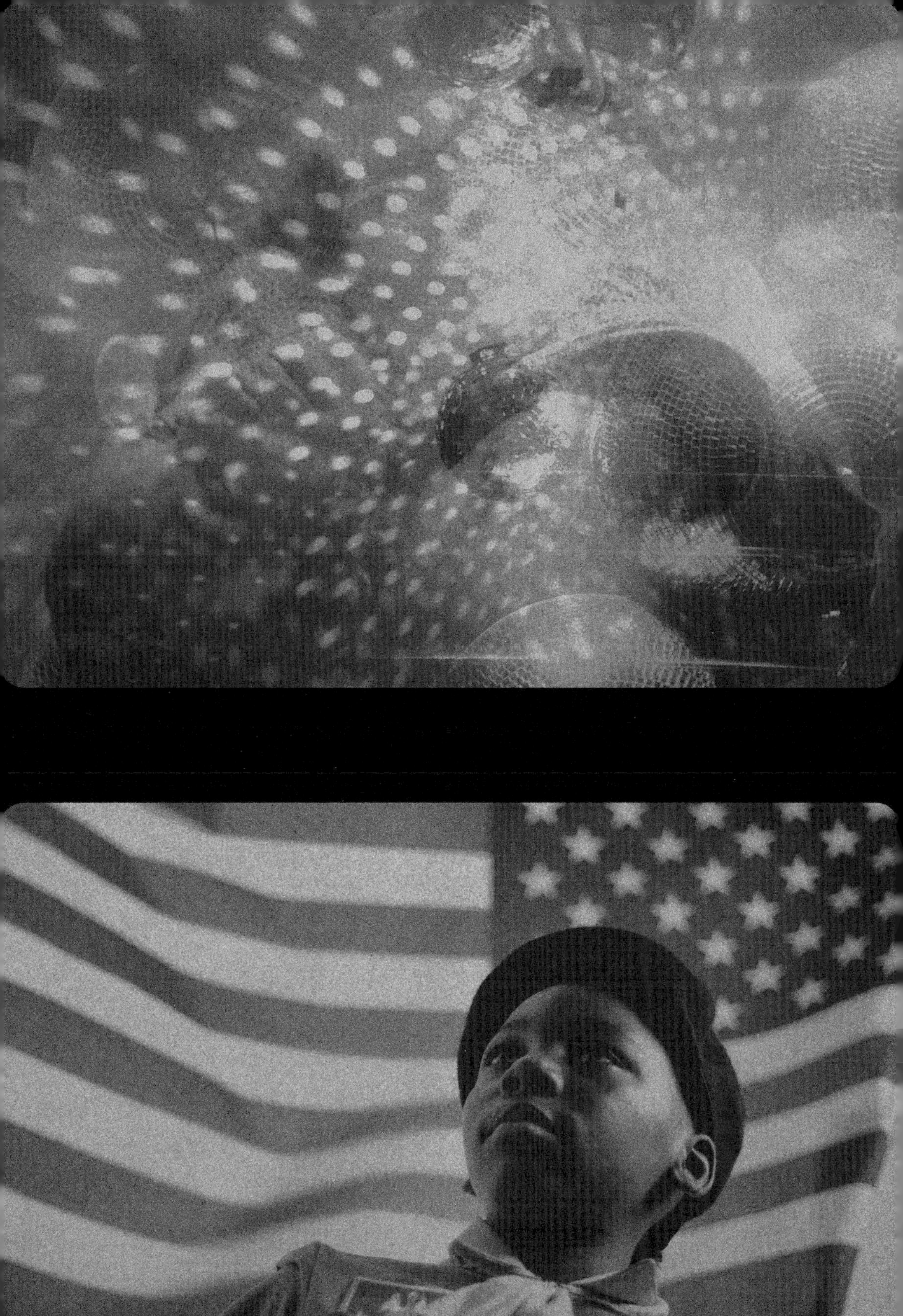
LOUISIANA

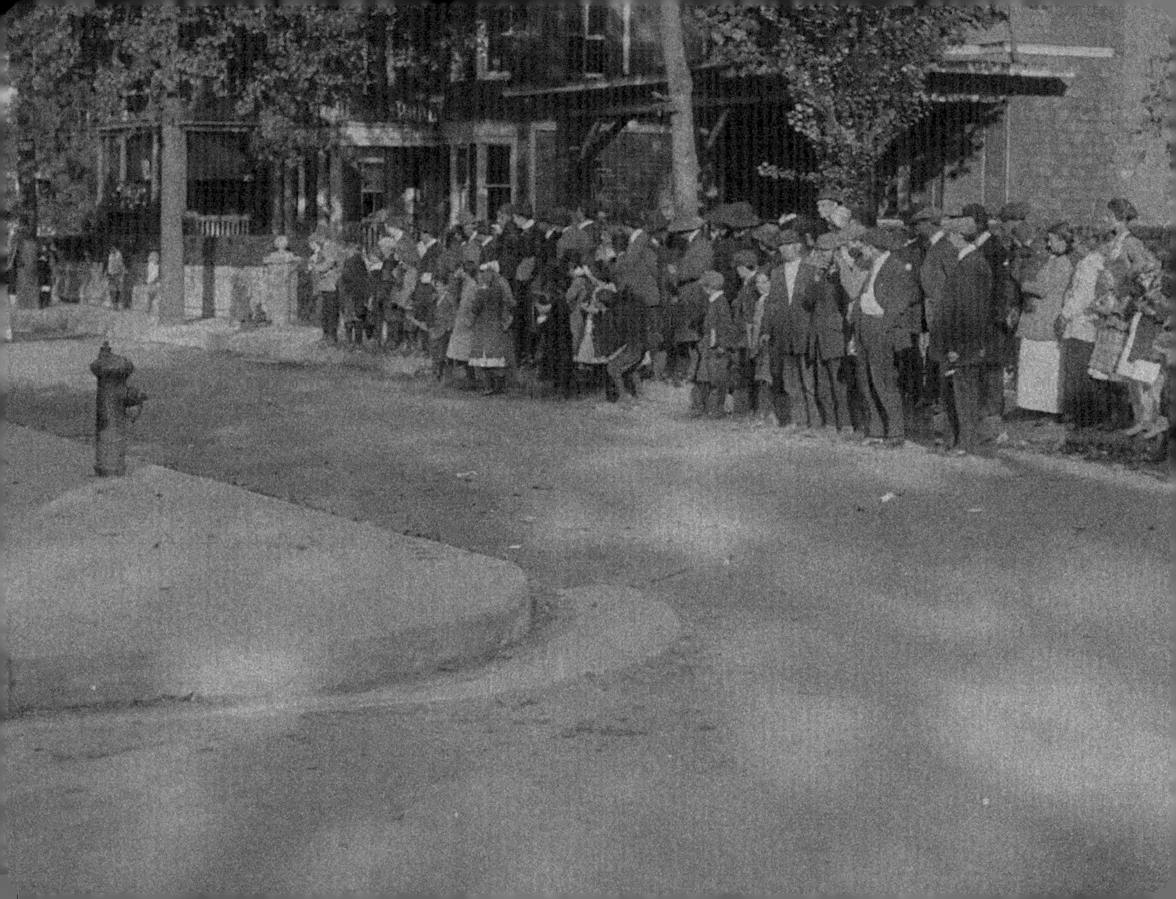

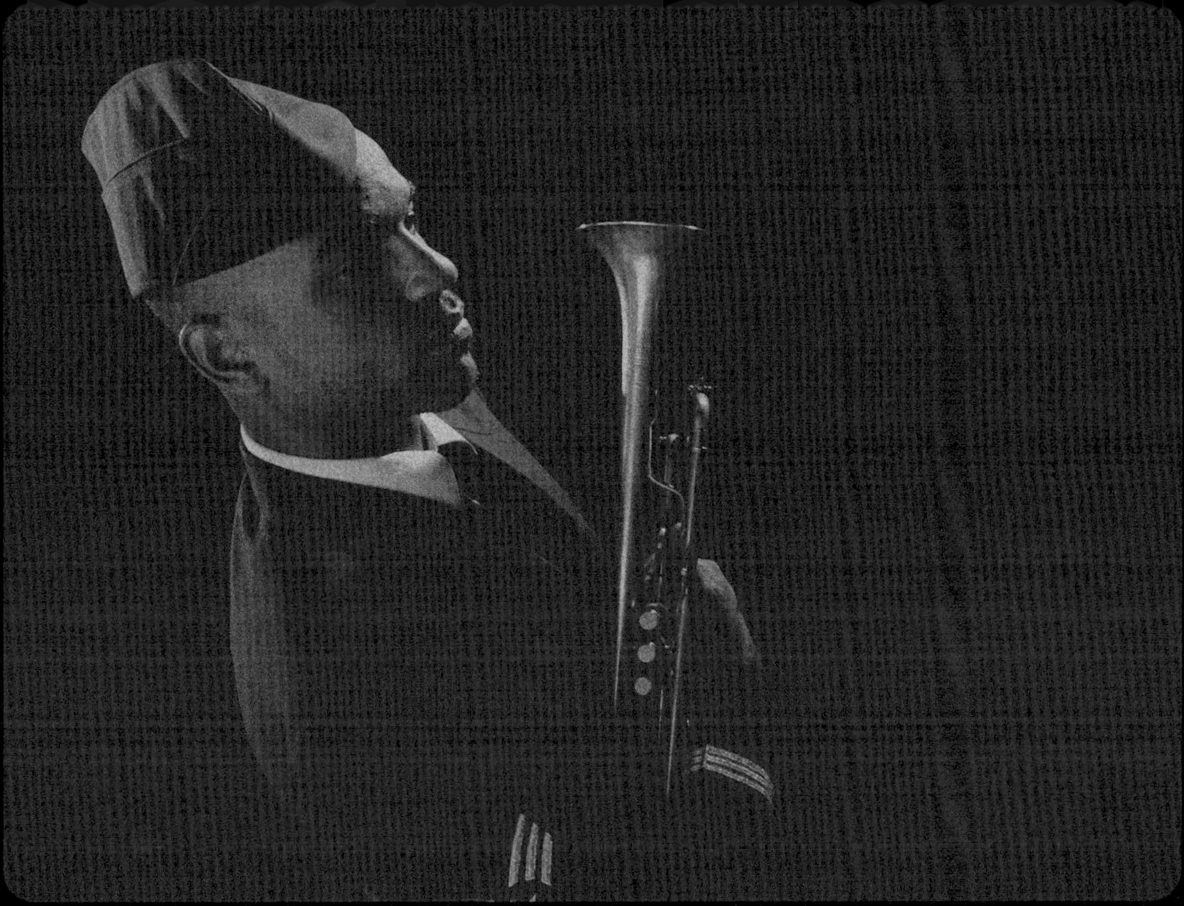

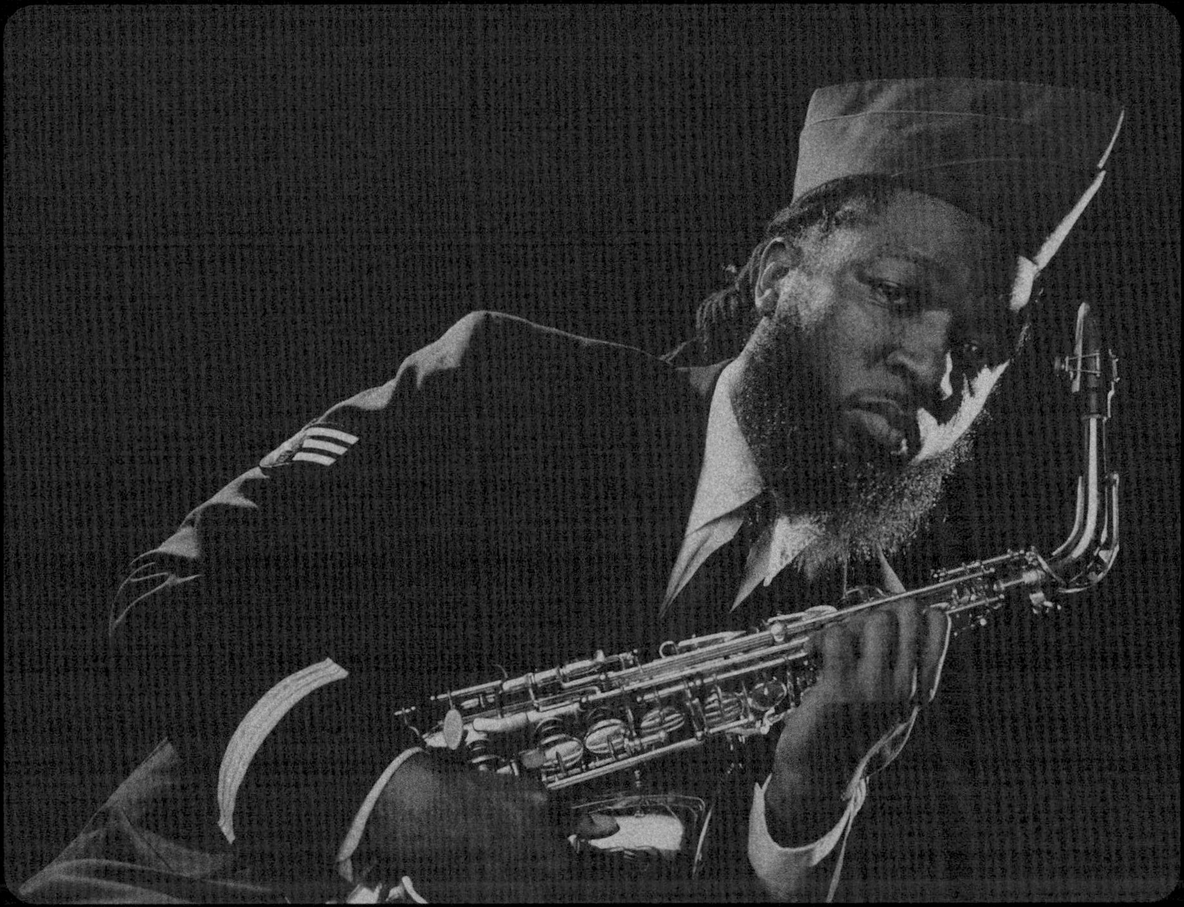

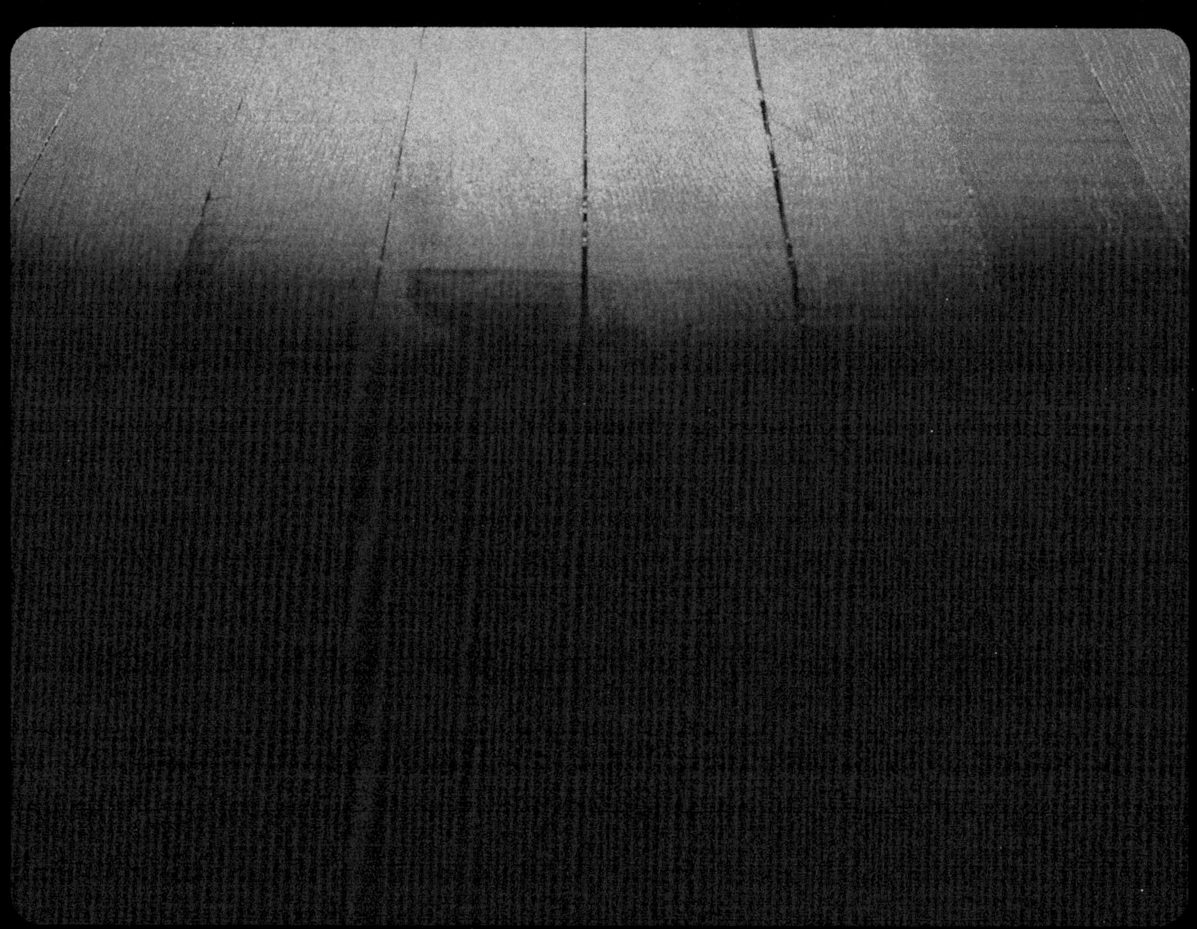

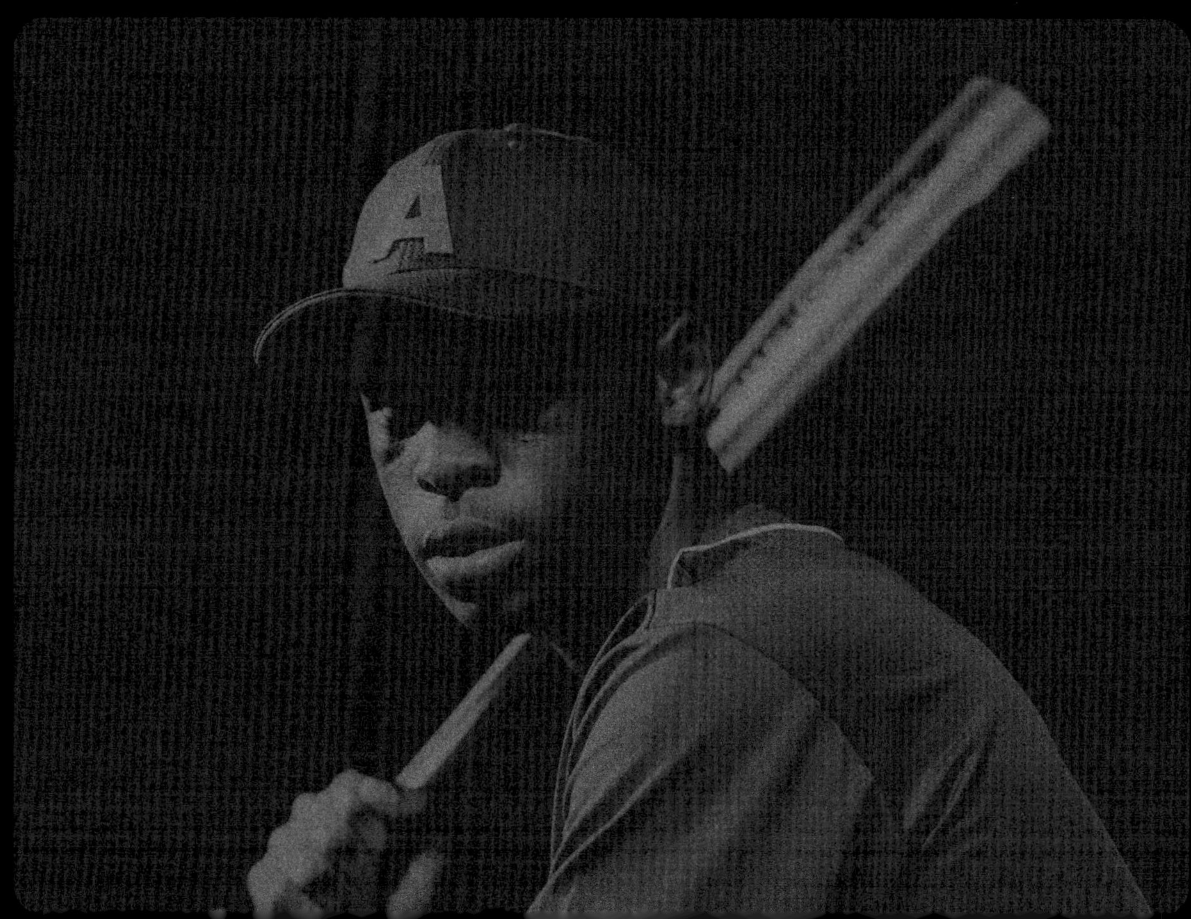

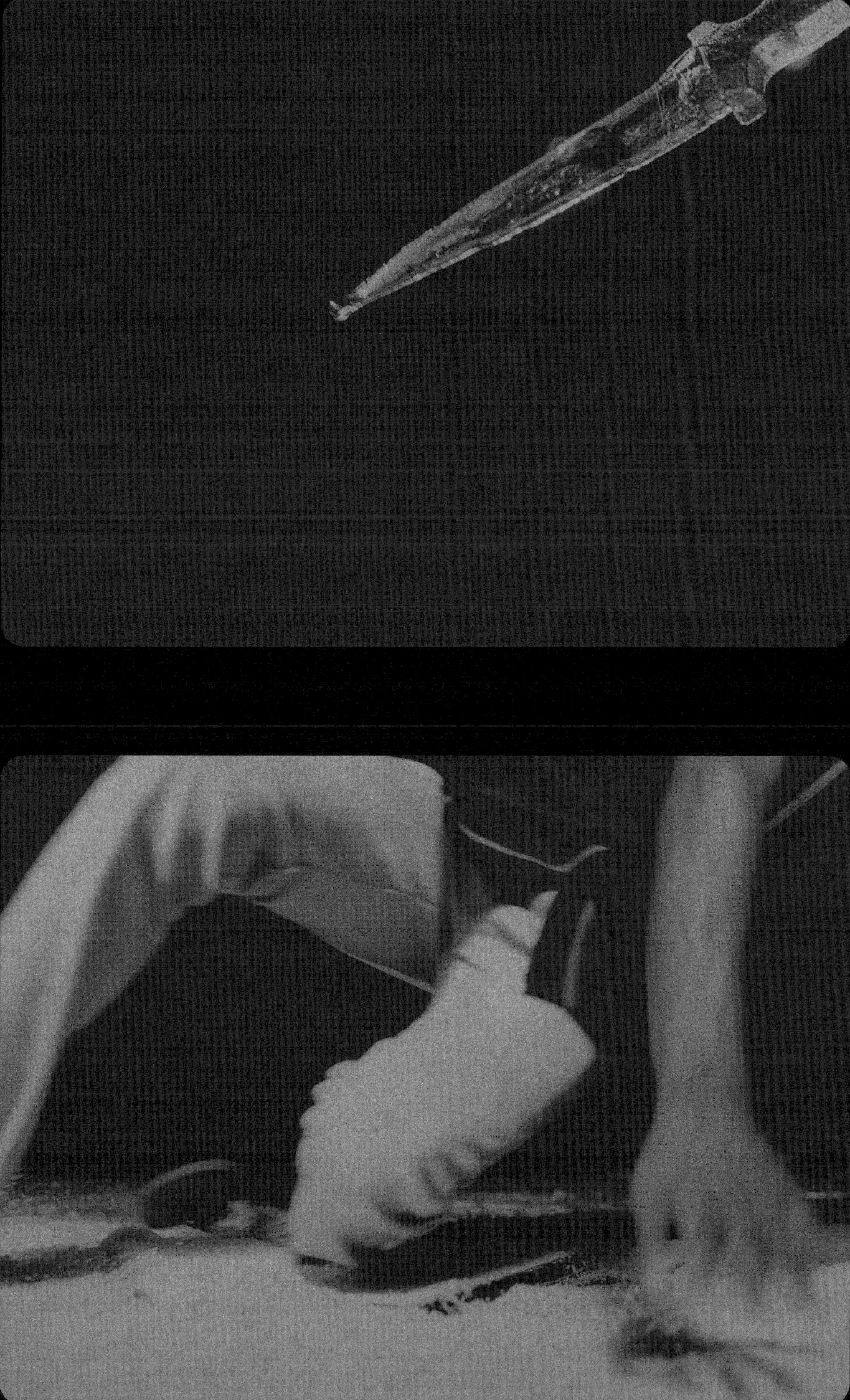

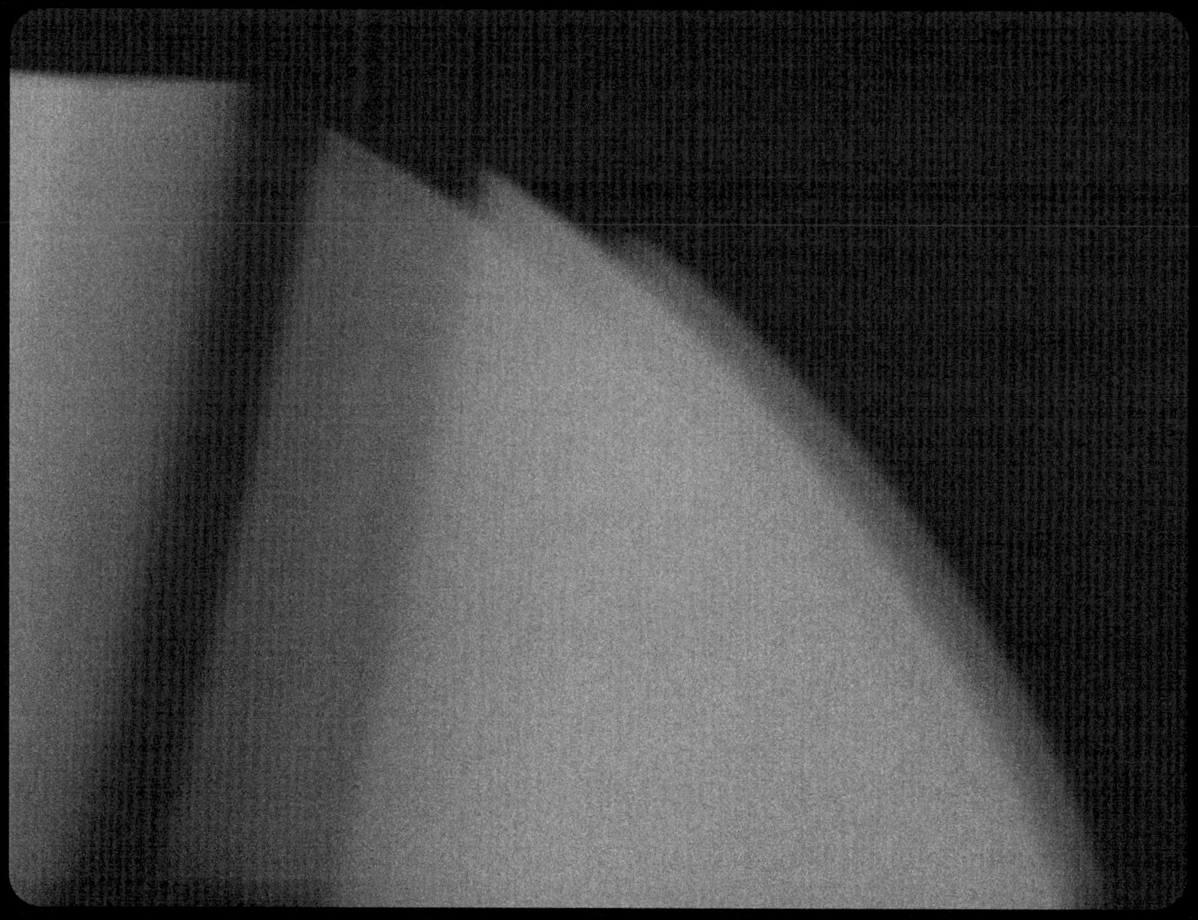

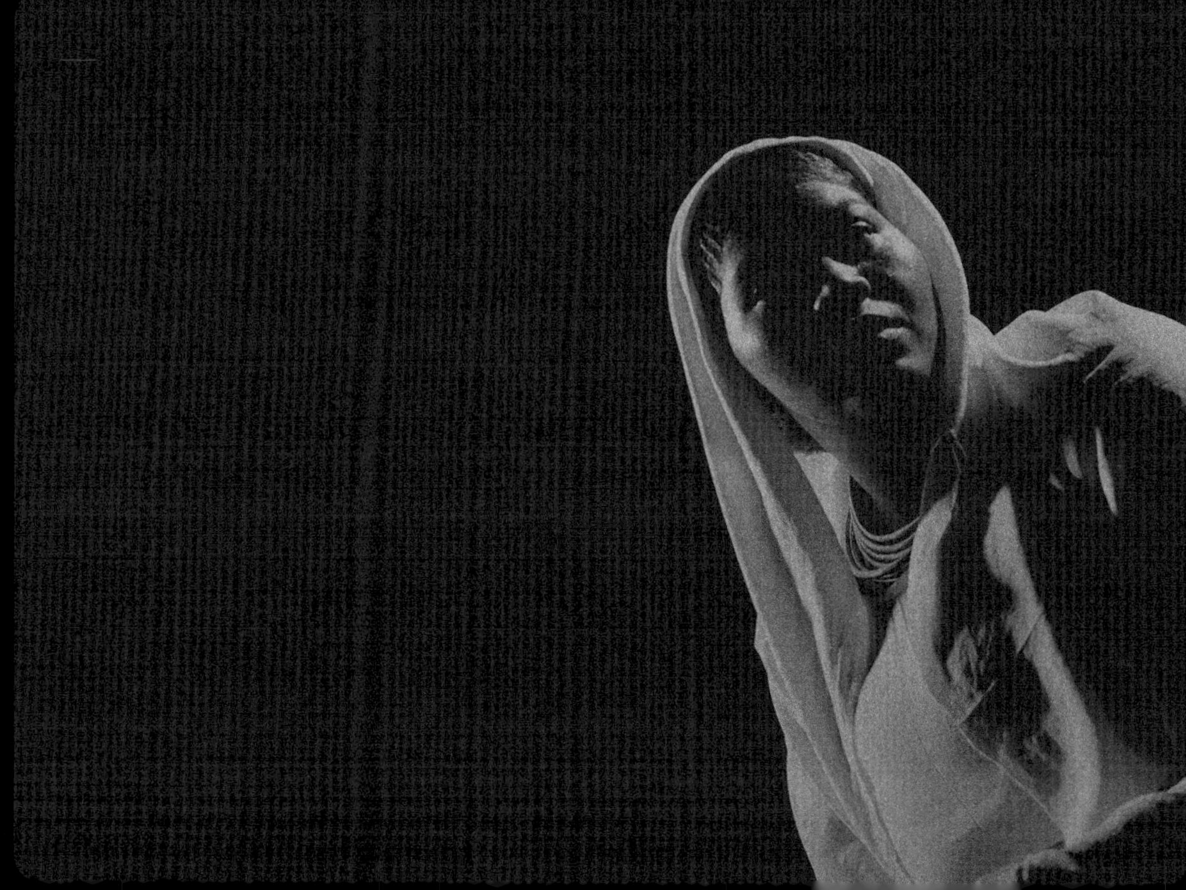

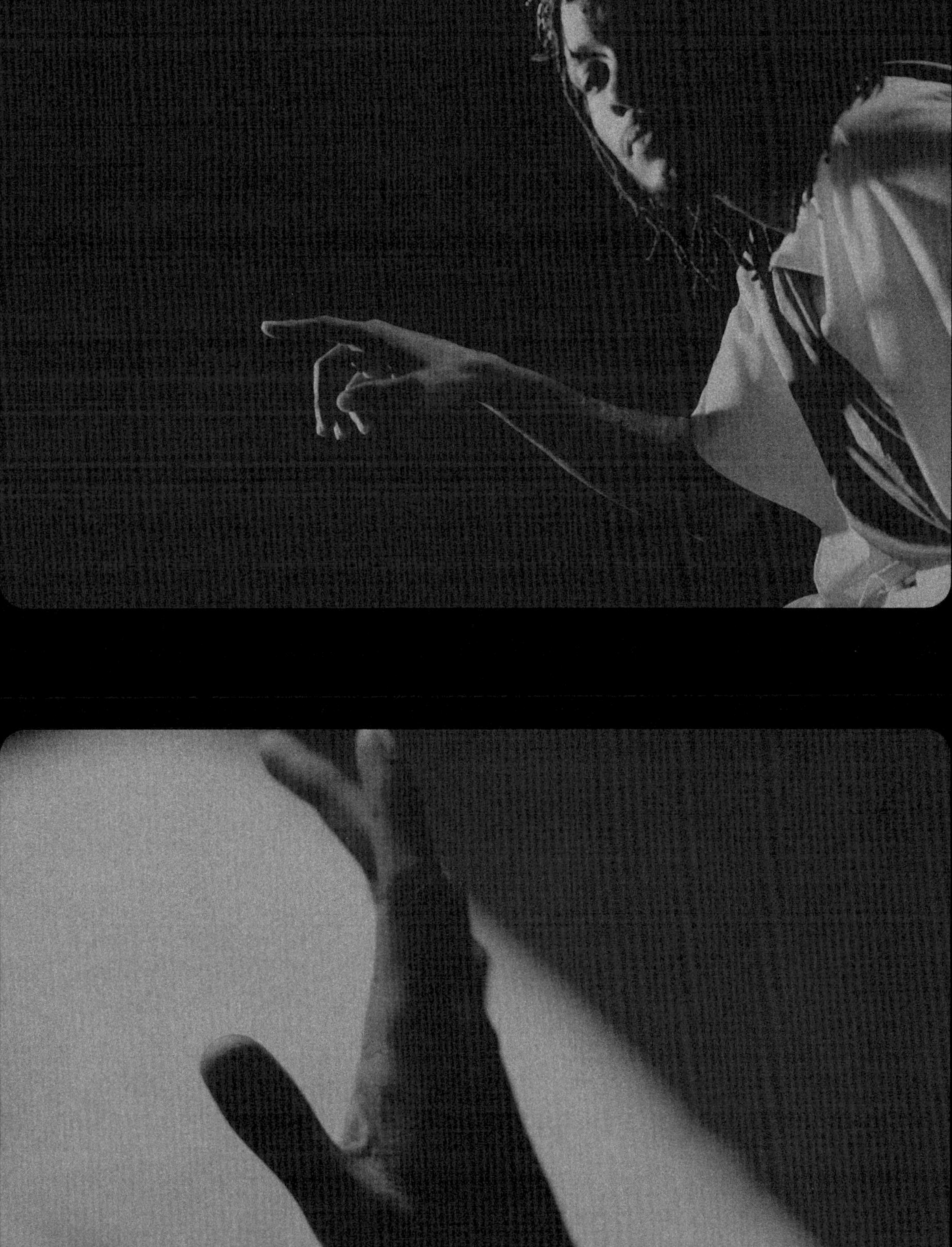

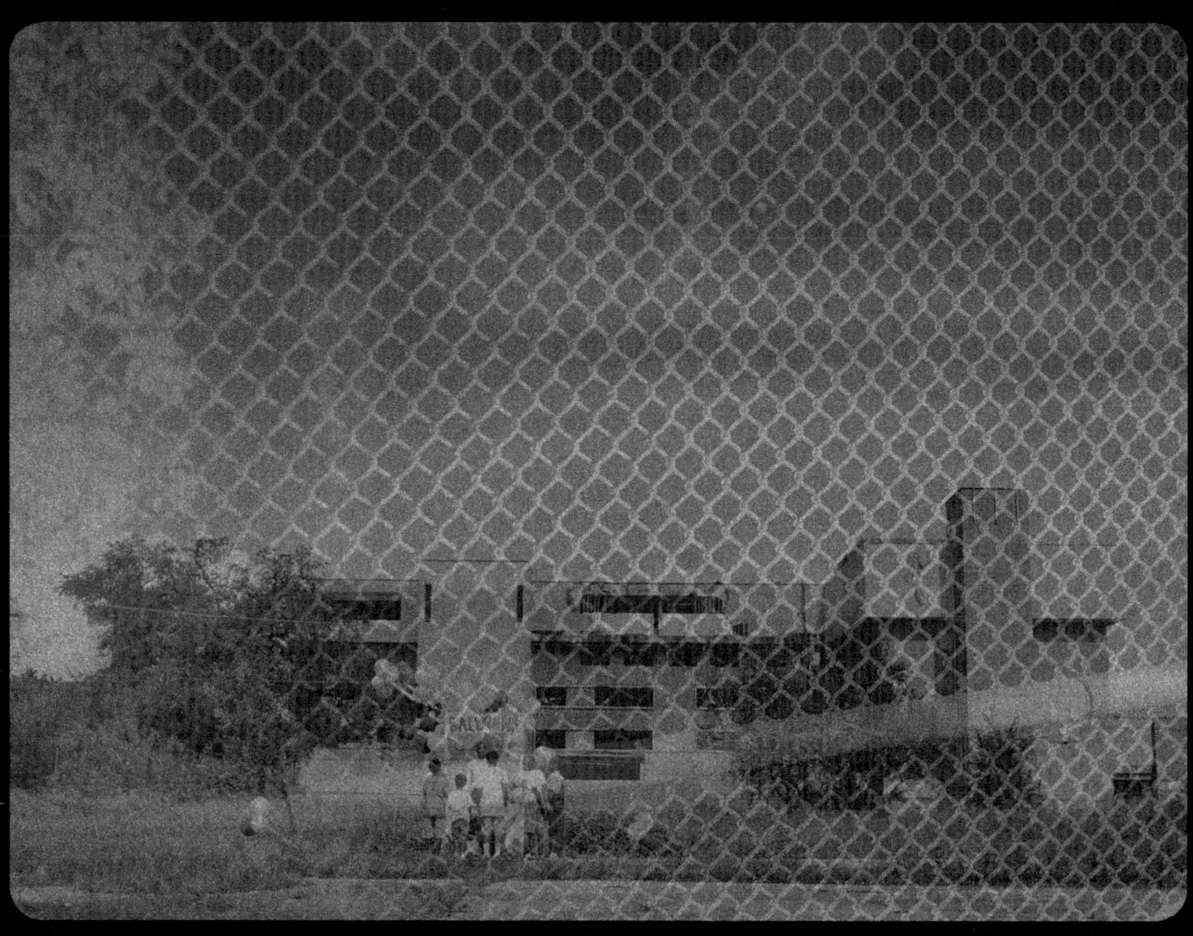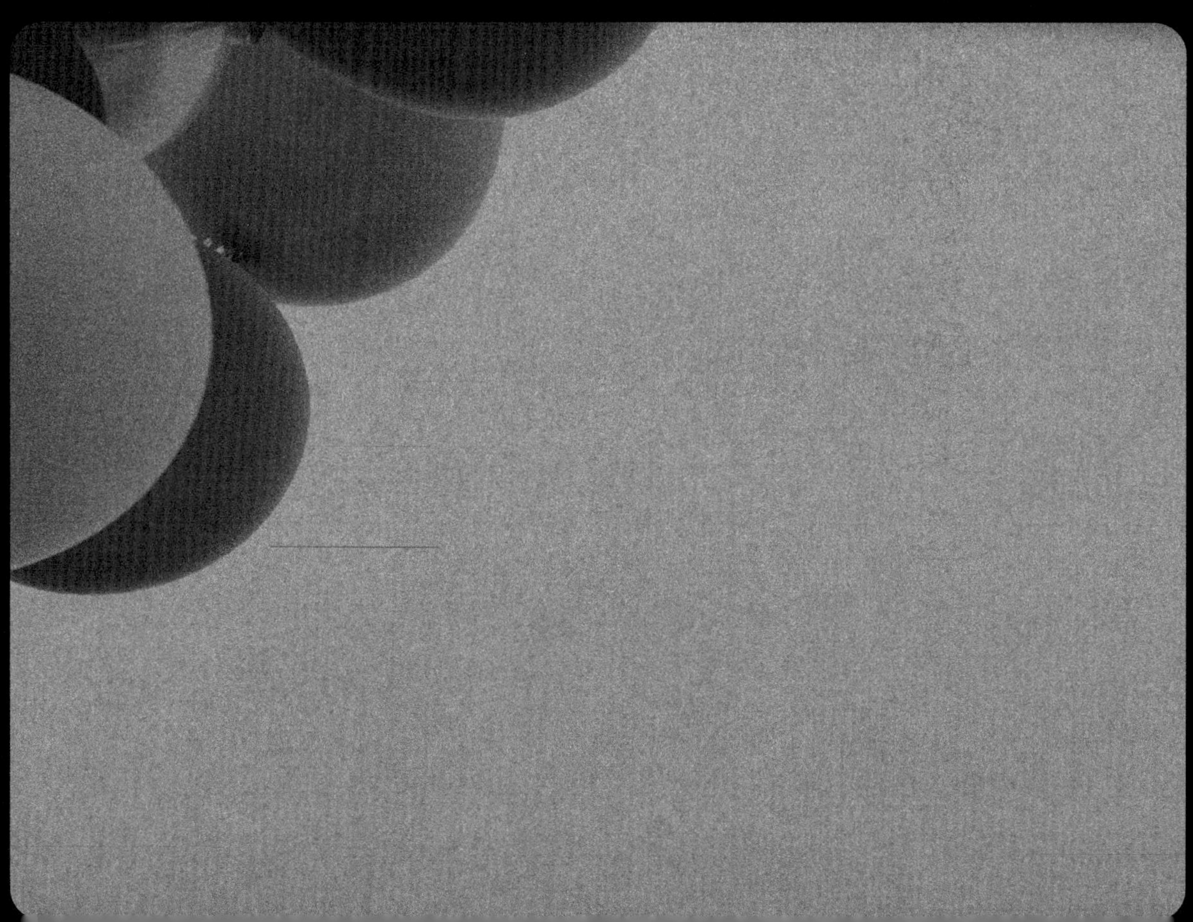

America

WOW

AKA

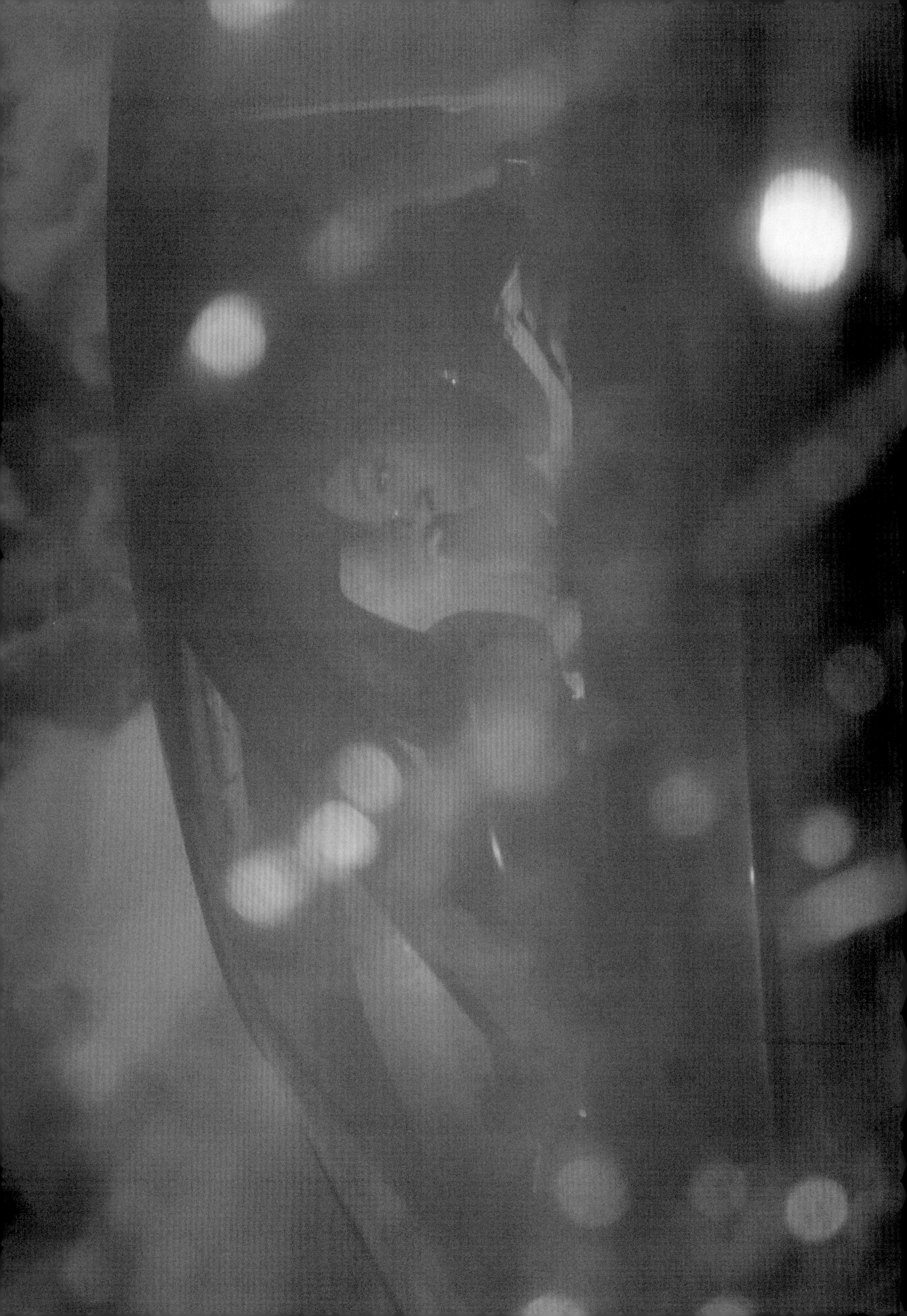

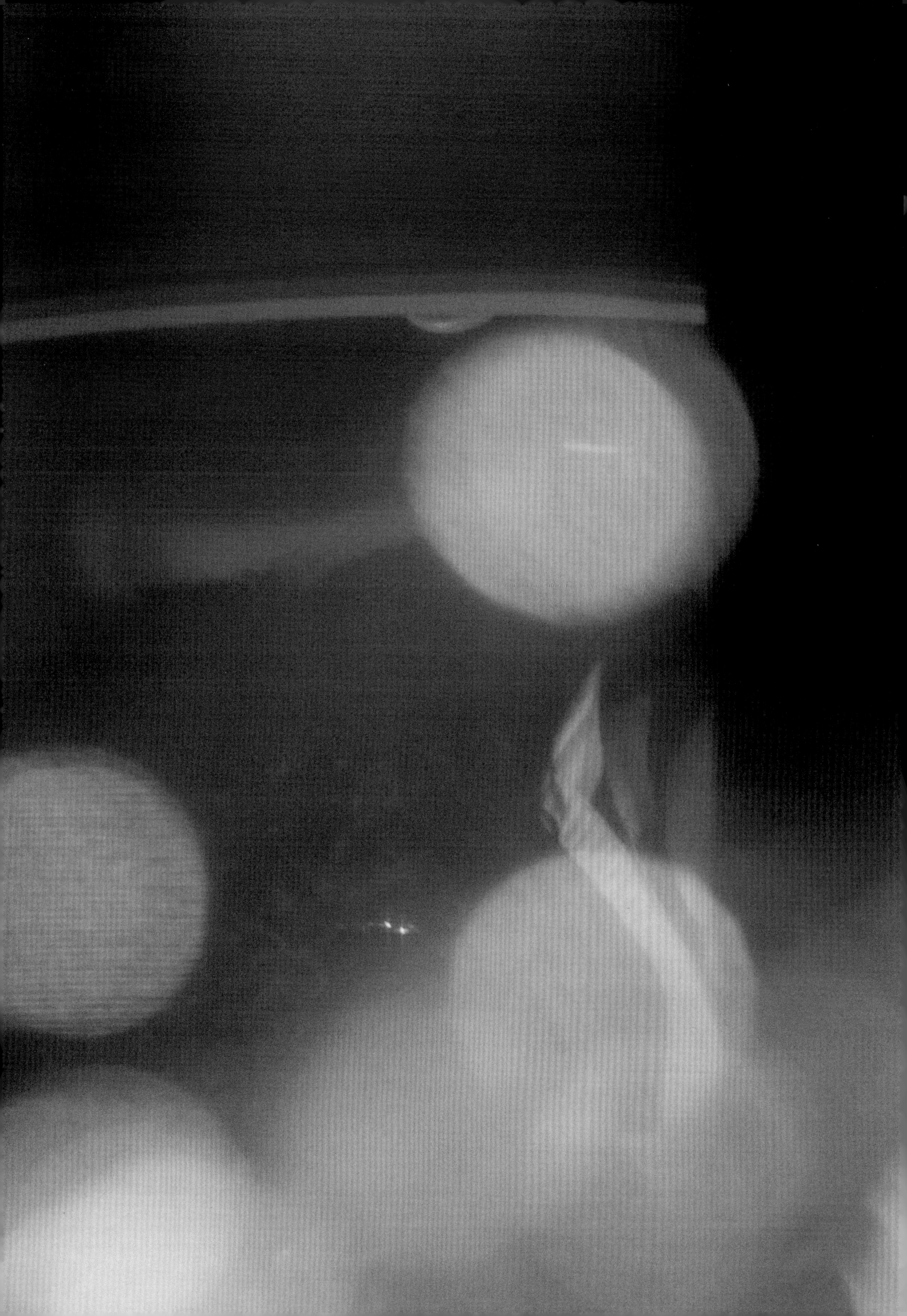

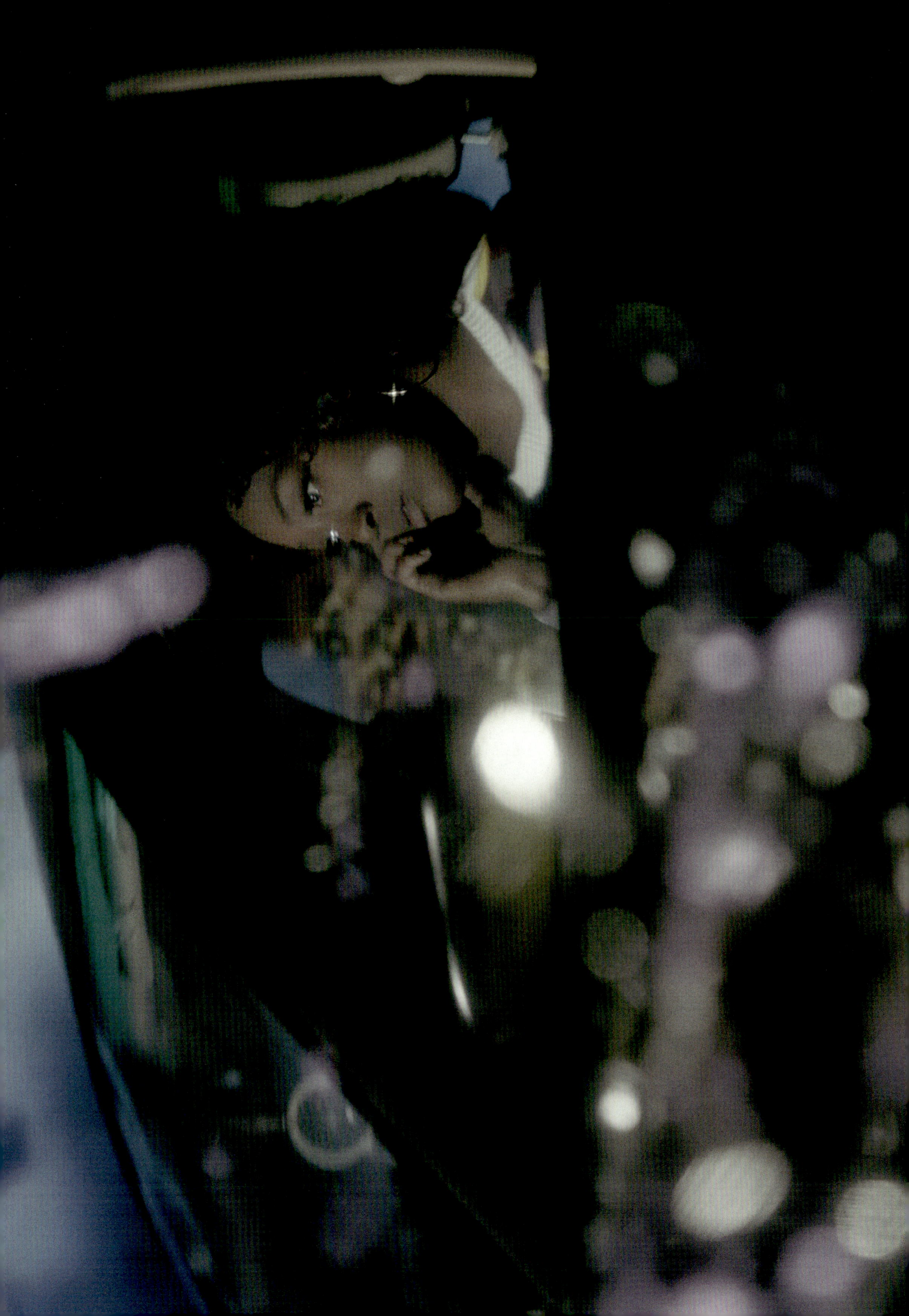

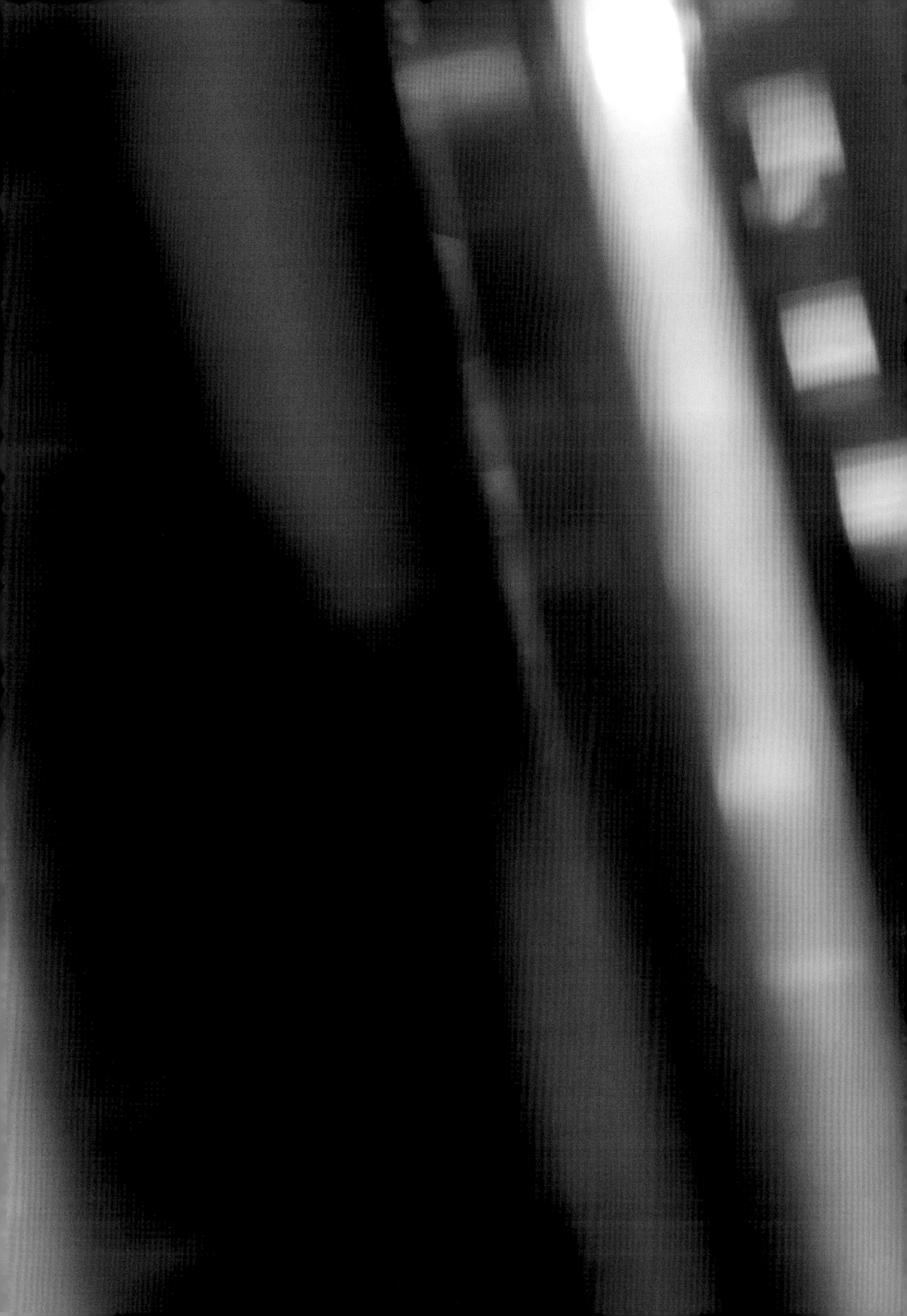

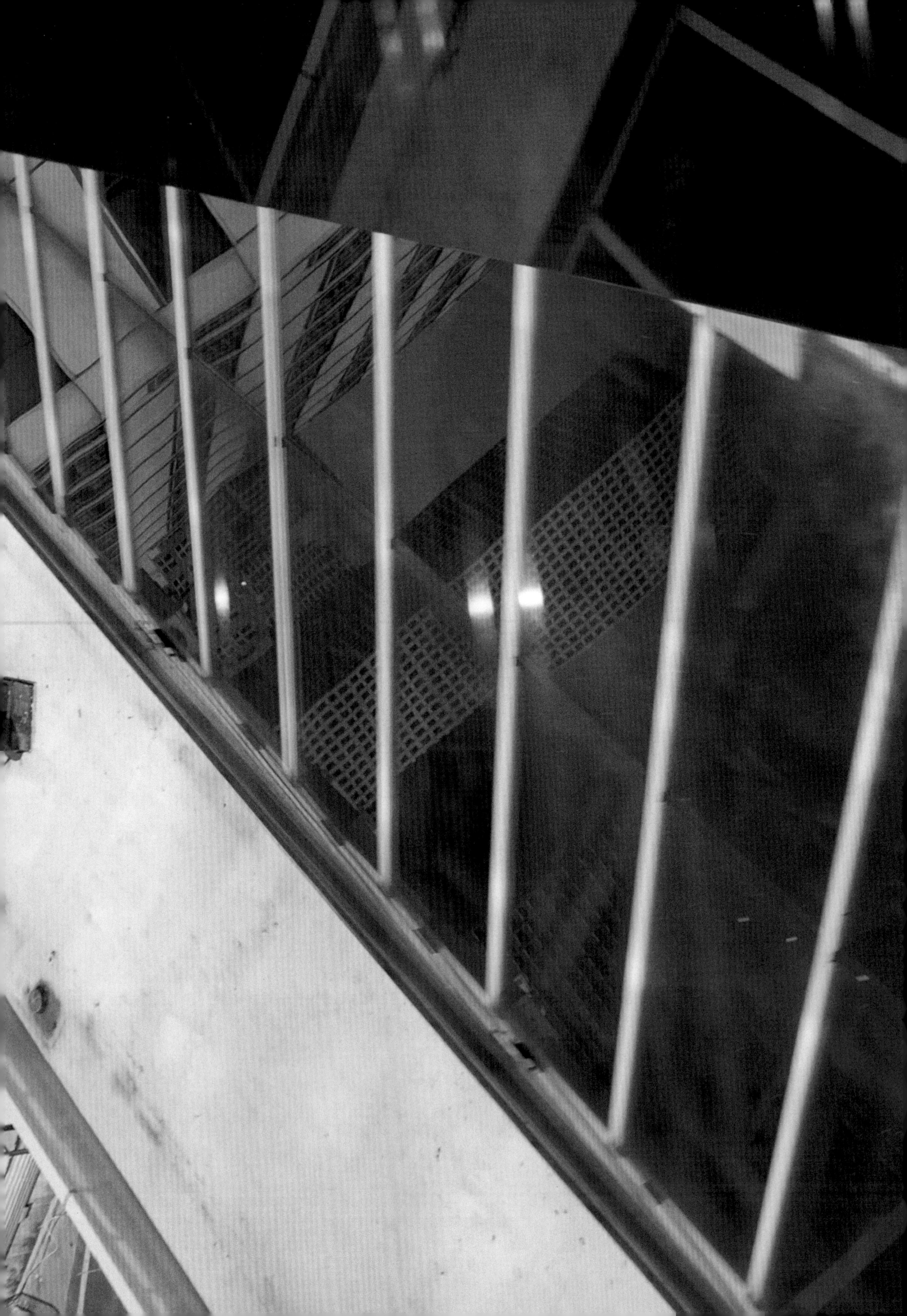

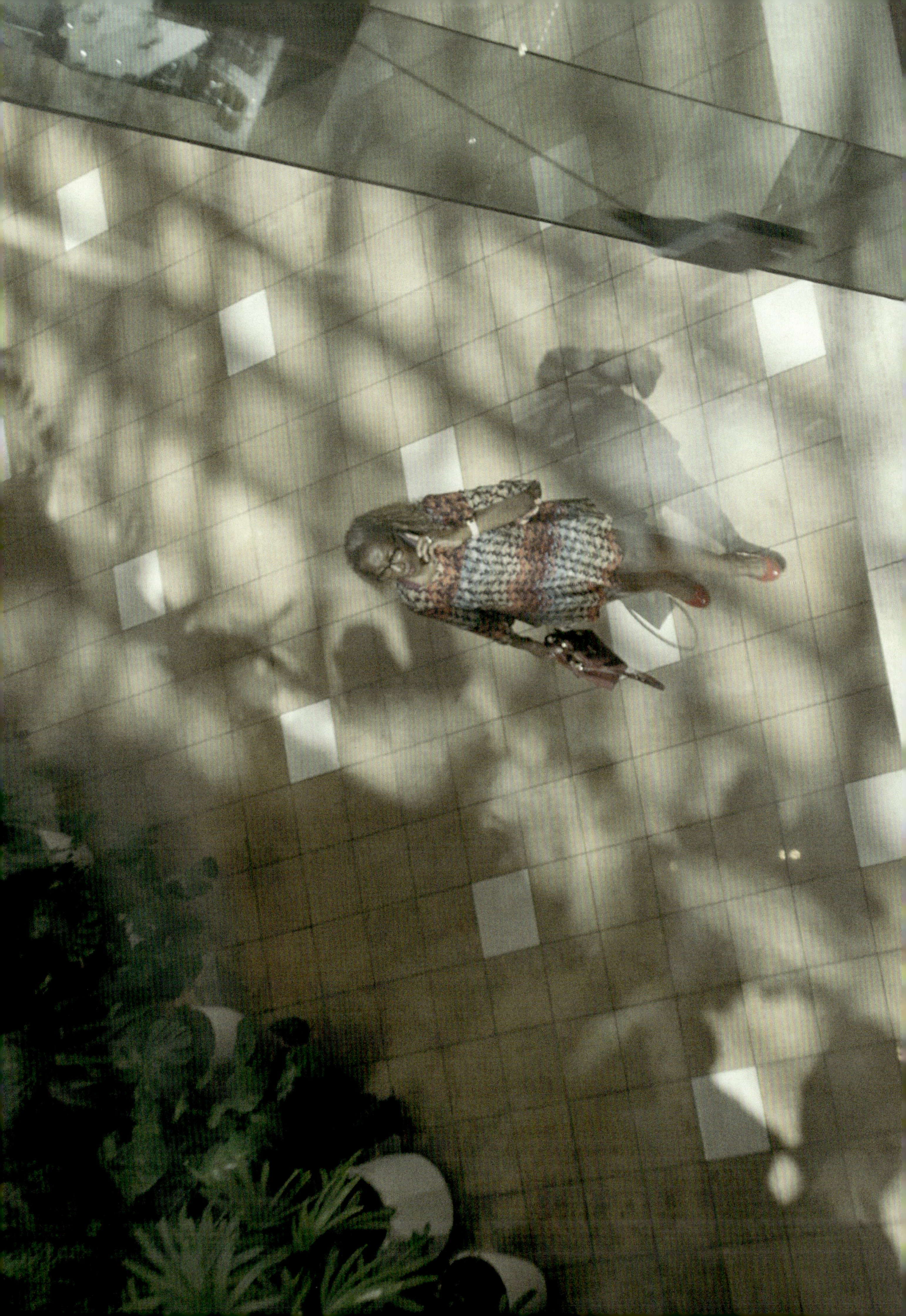

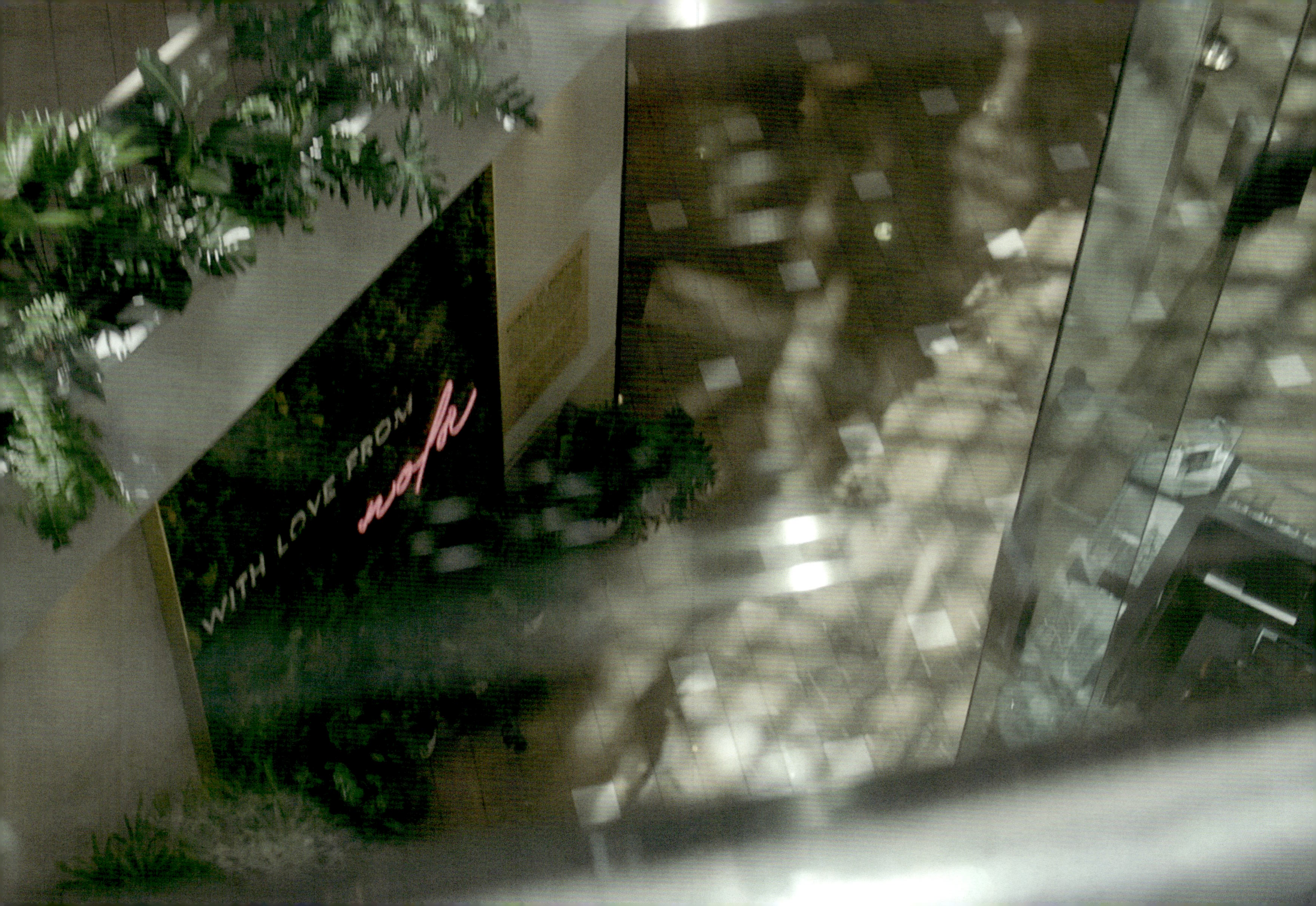

WITH LOVE FROM

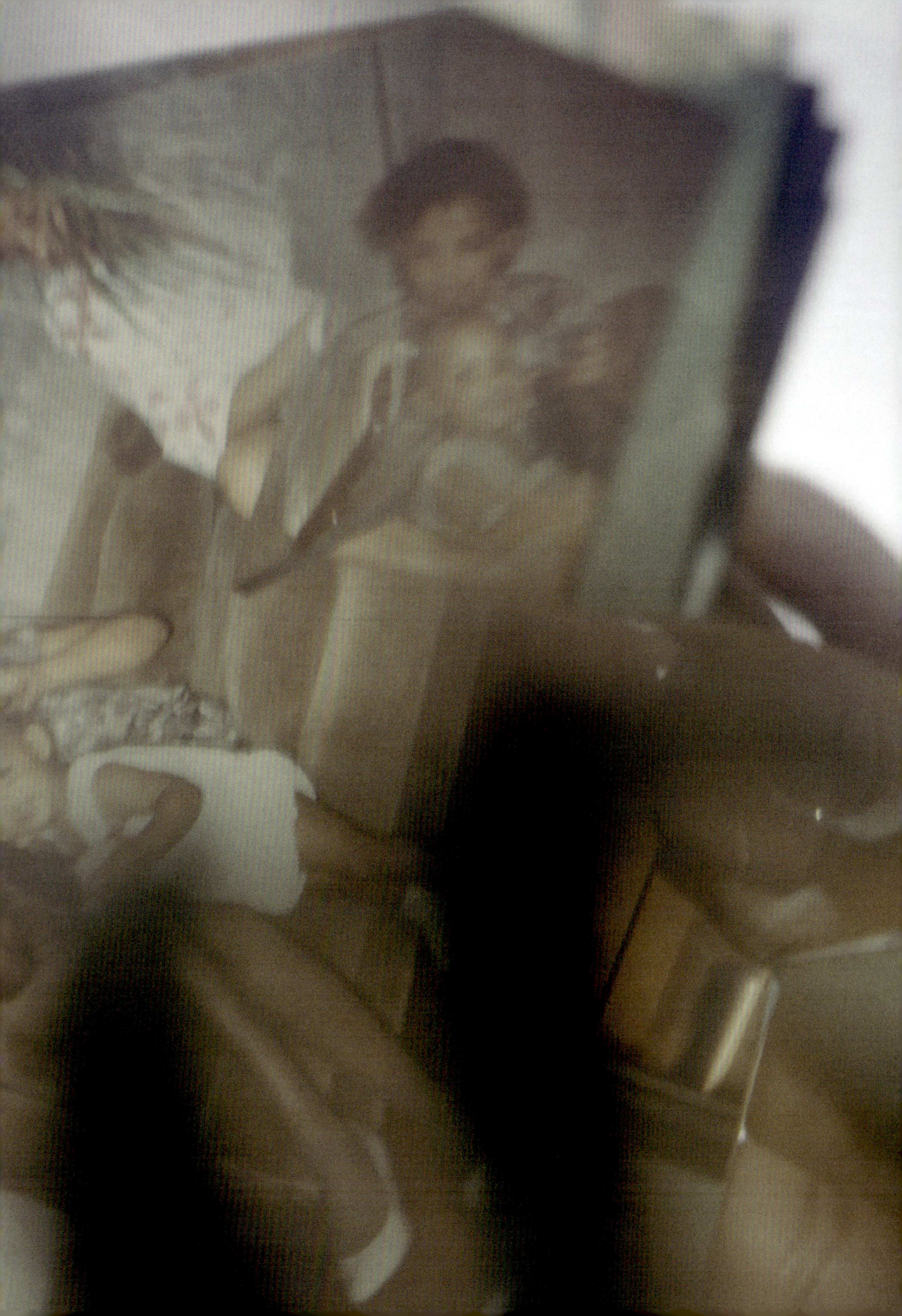

Are you colour struck?

Am I colour struck?

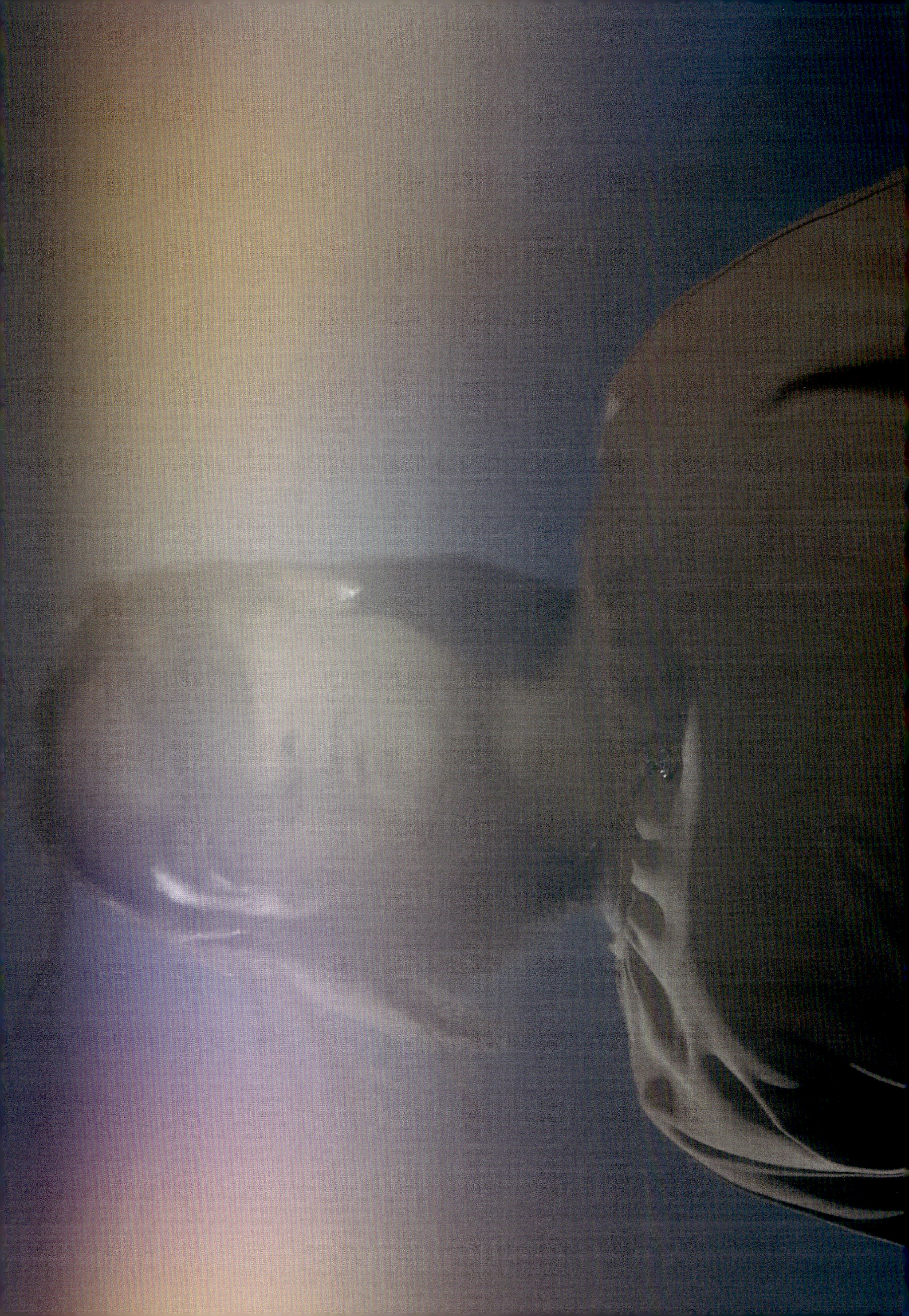

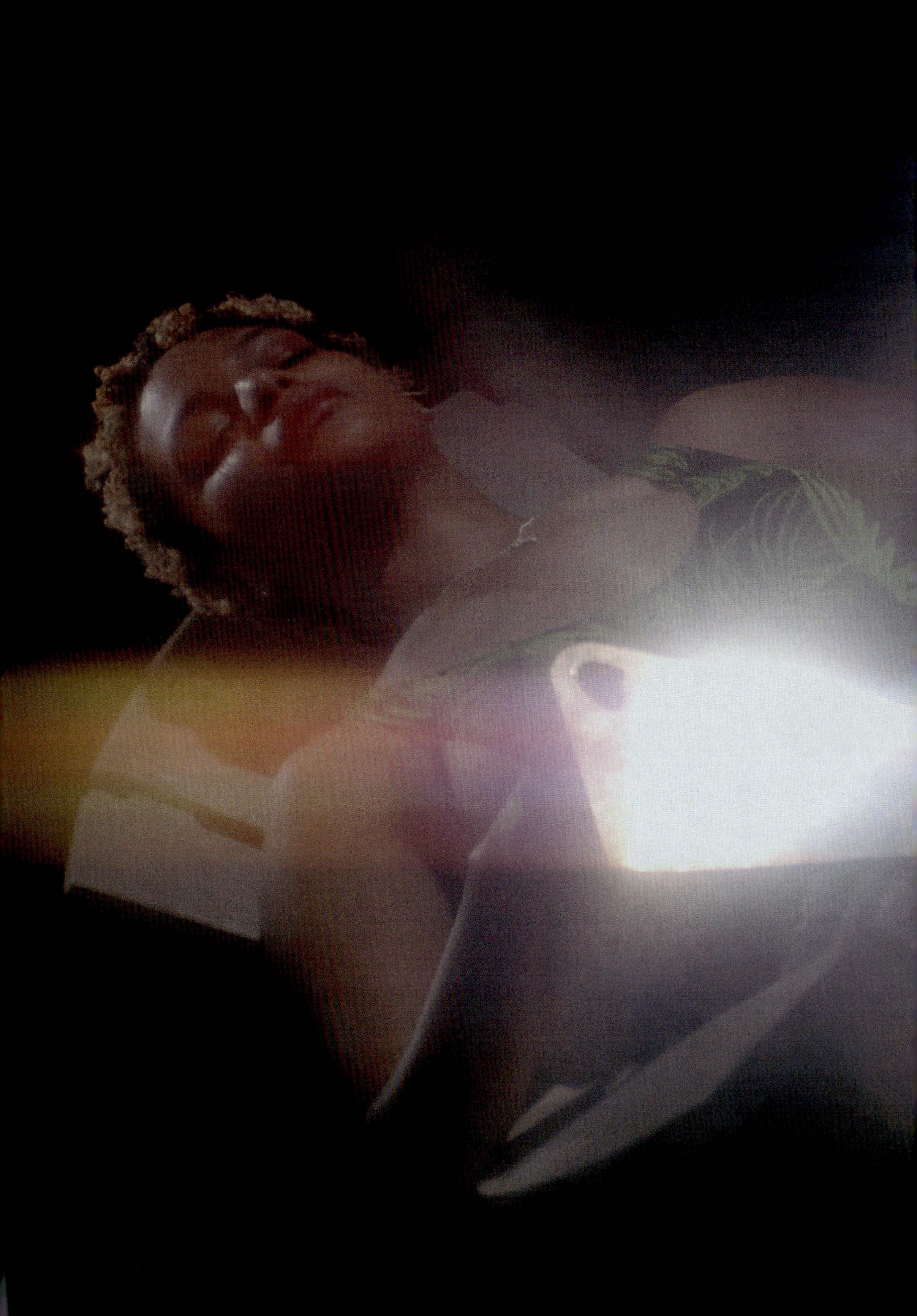

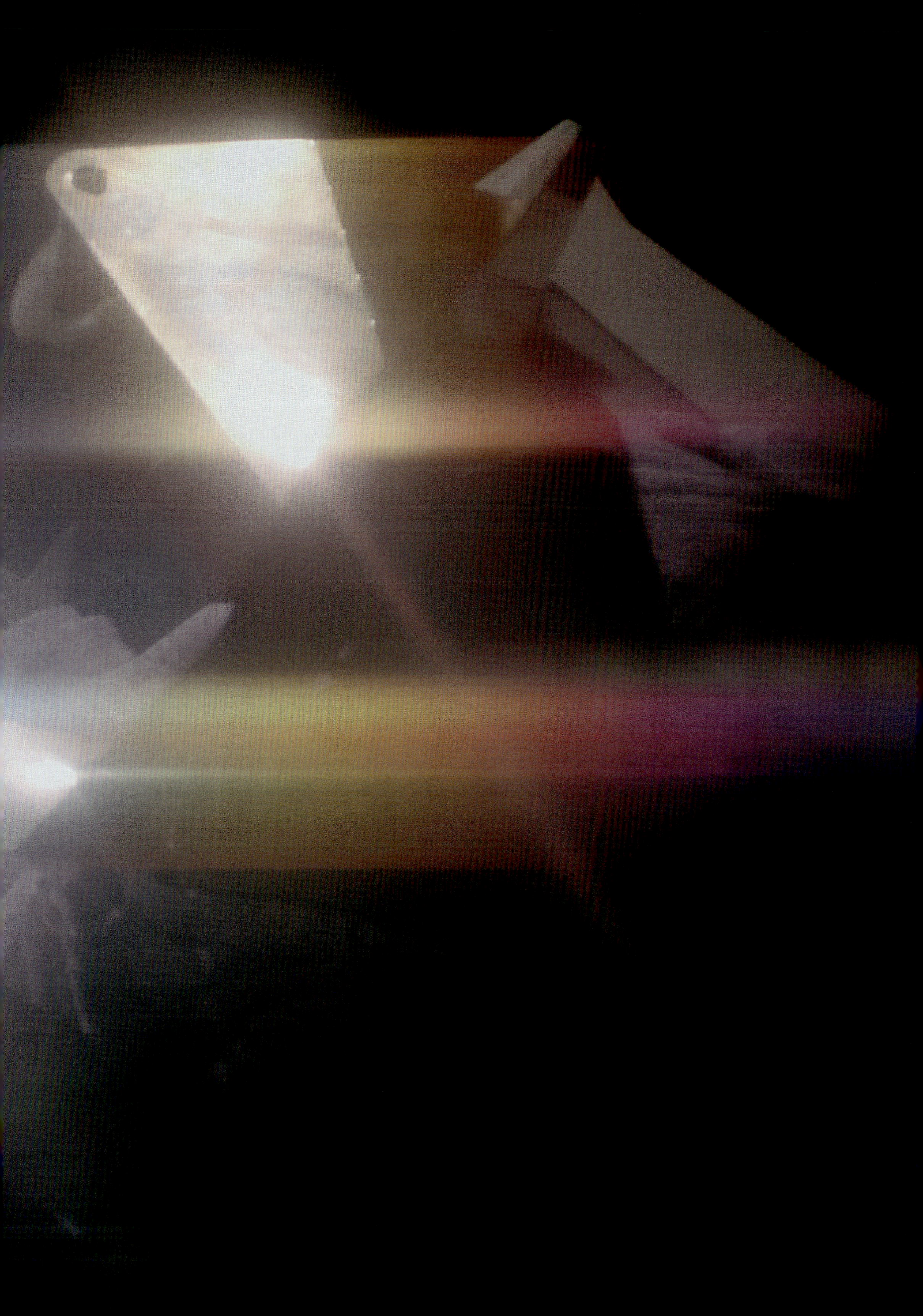

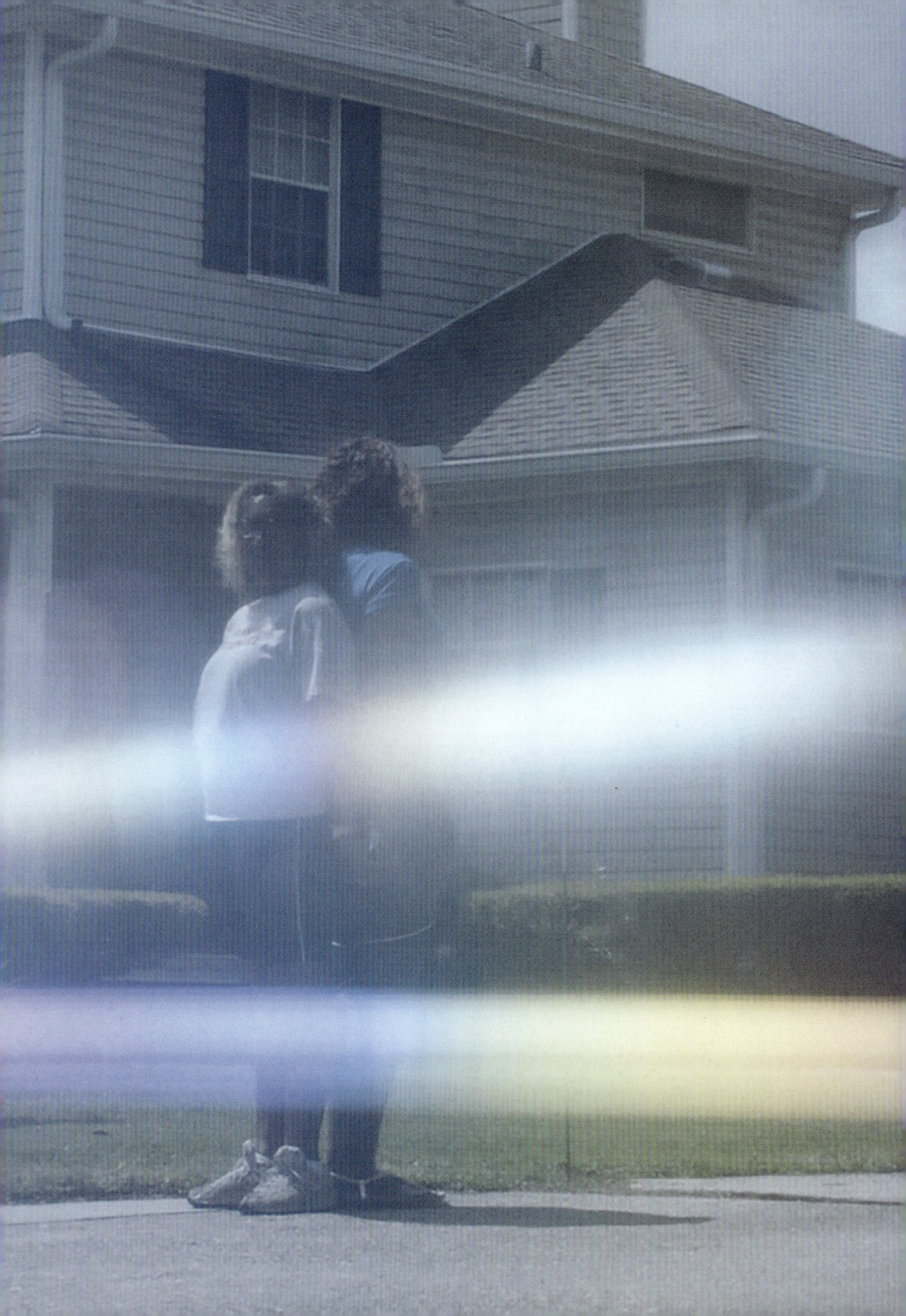

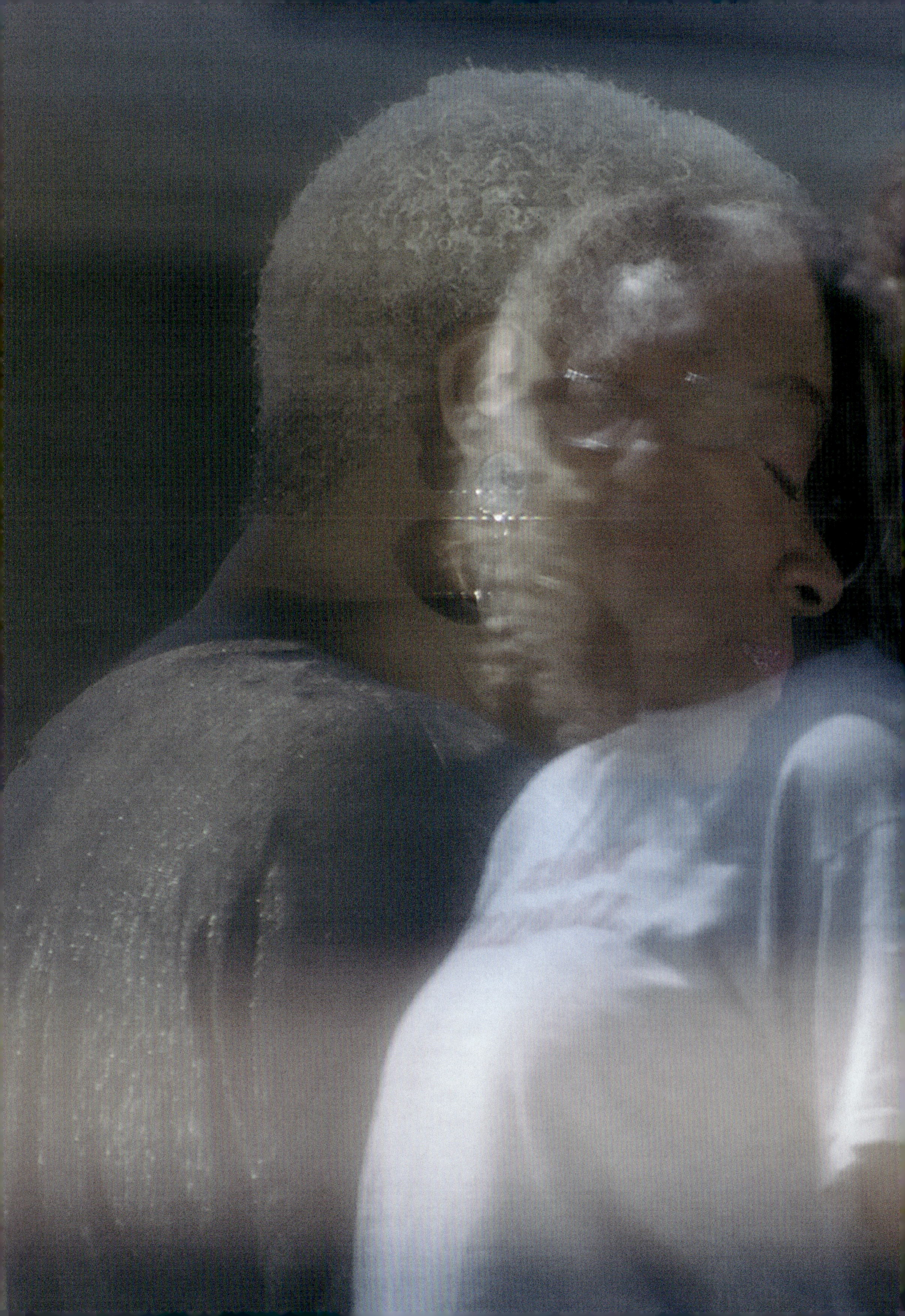

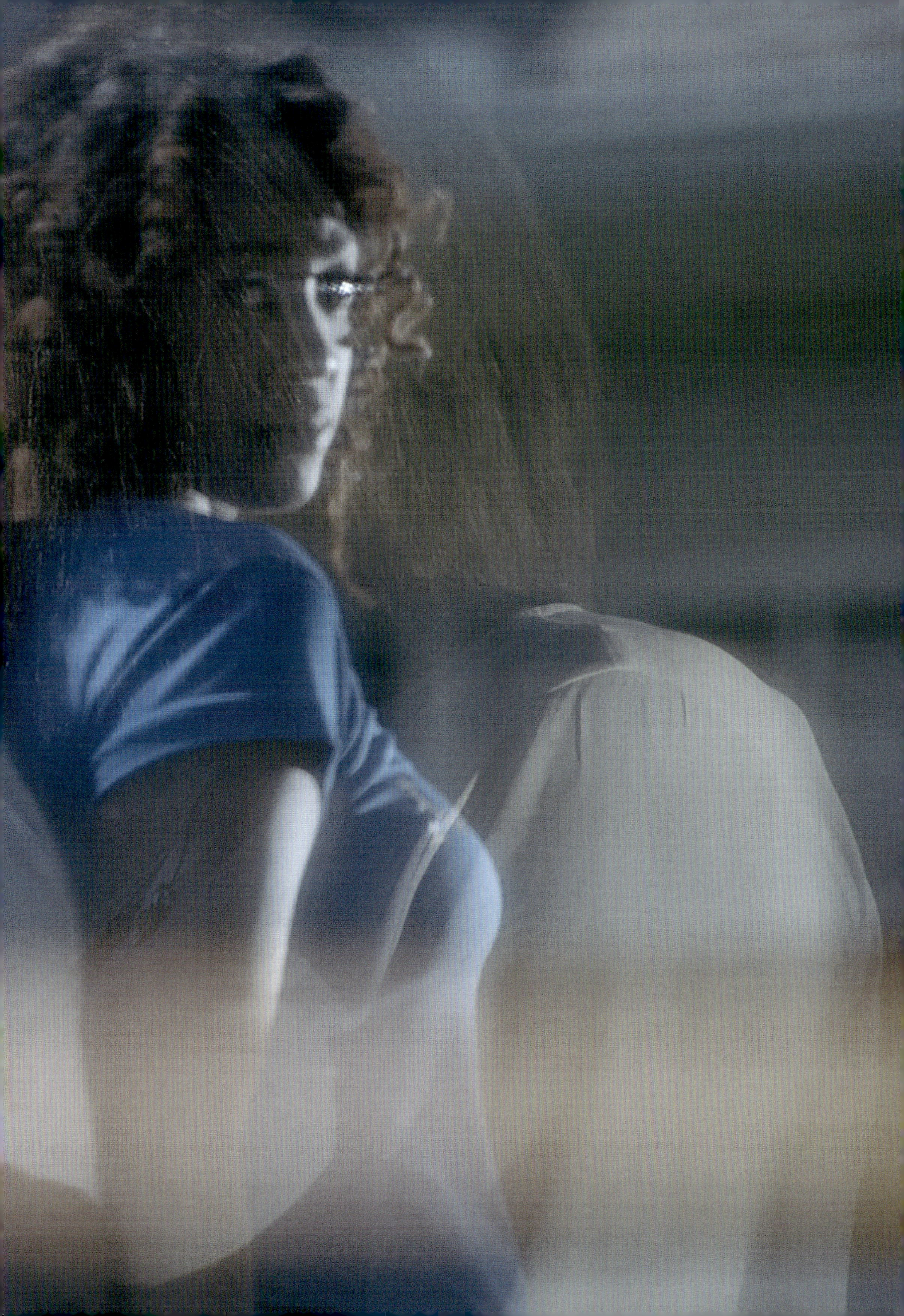

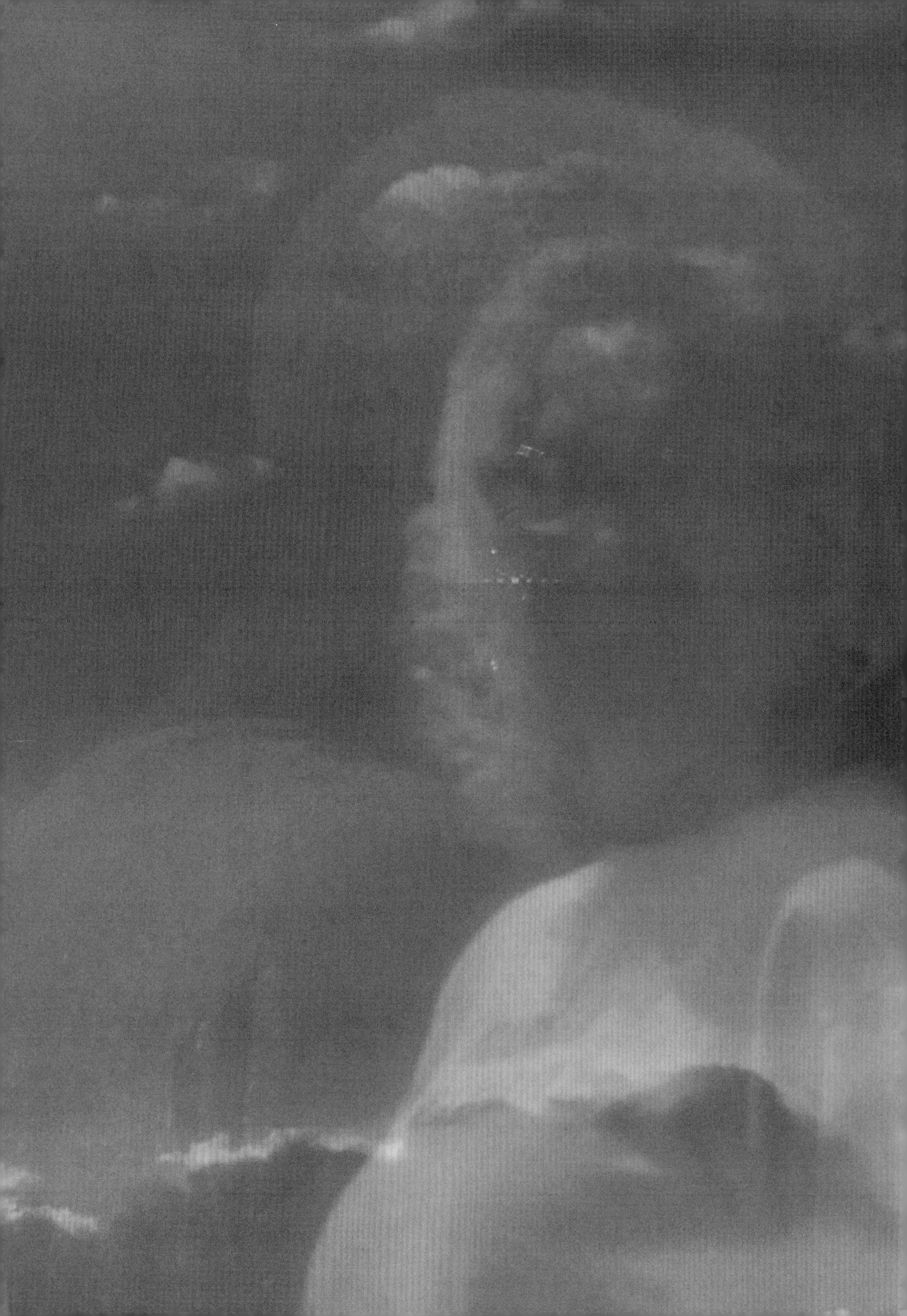

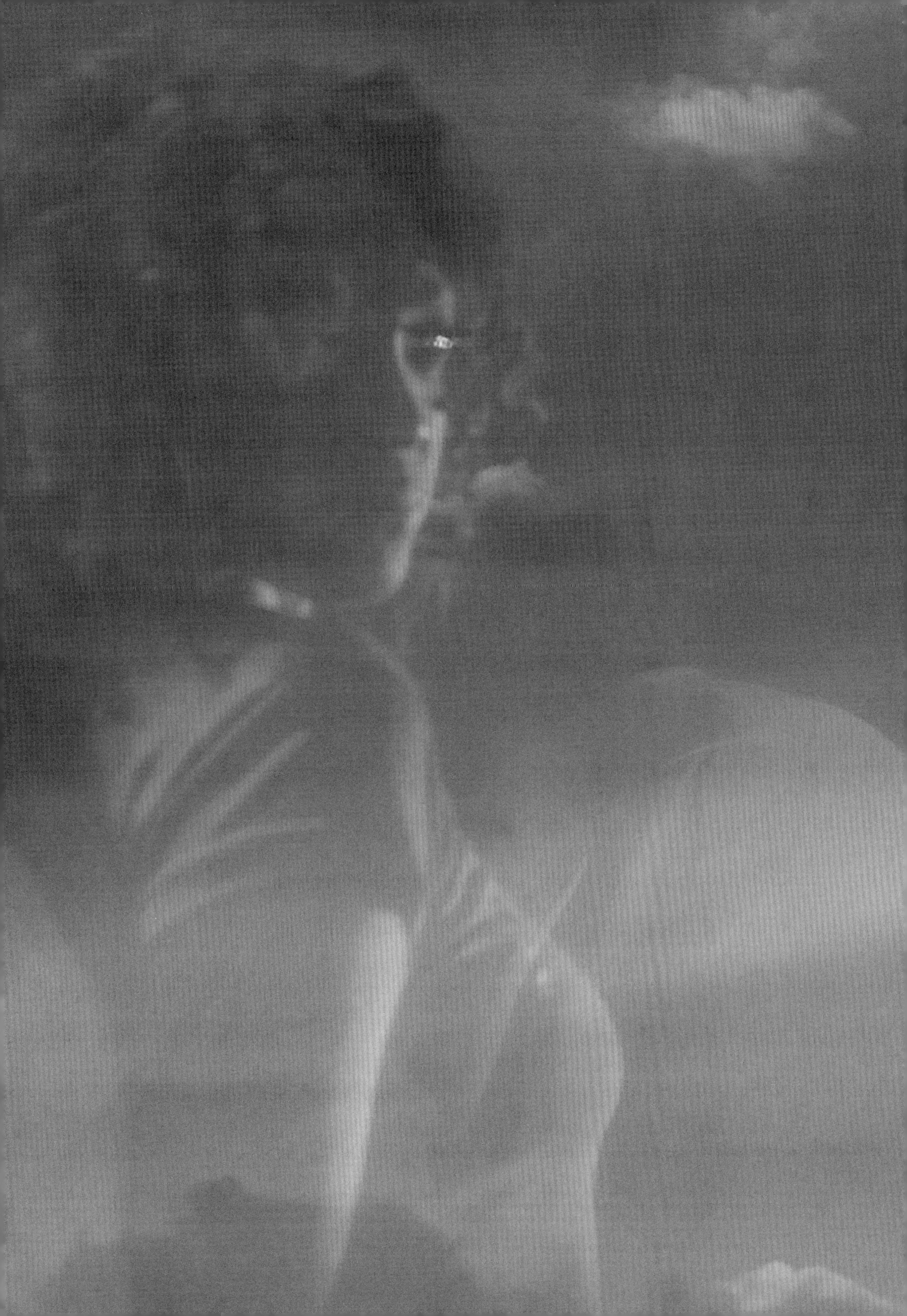

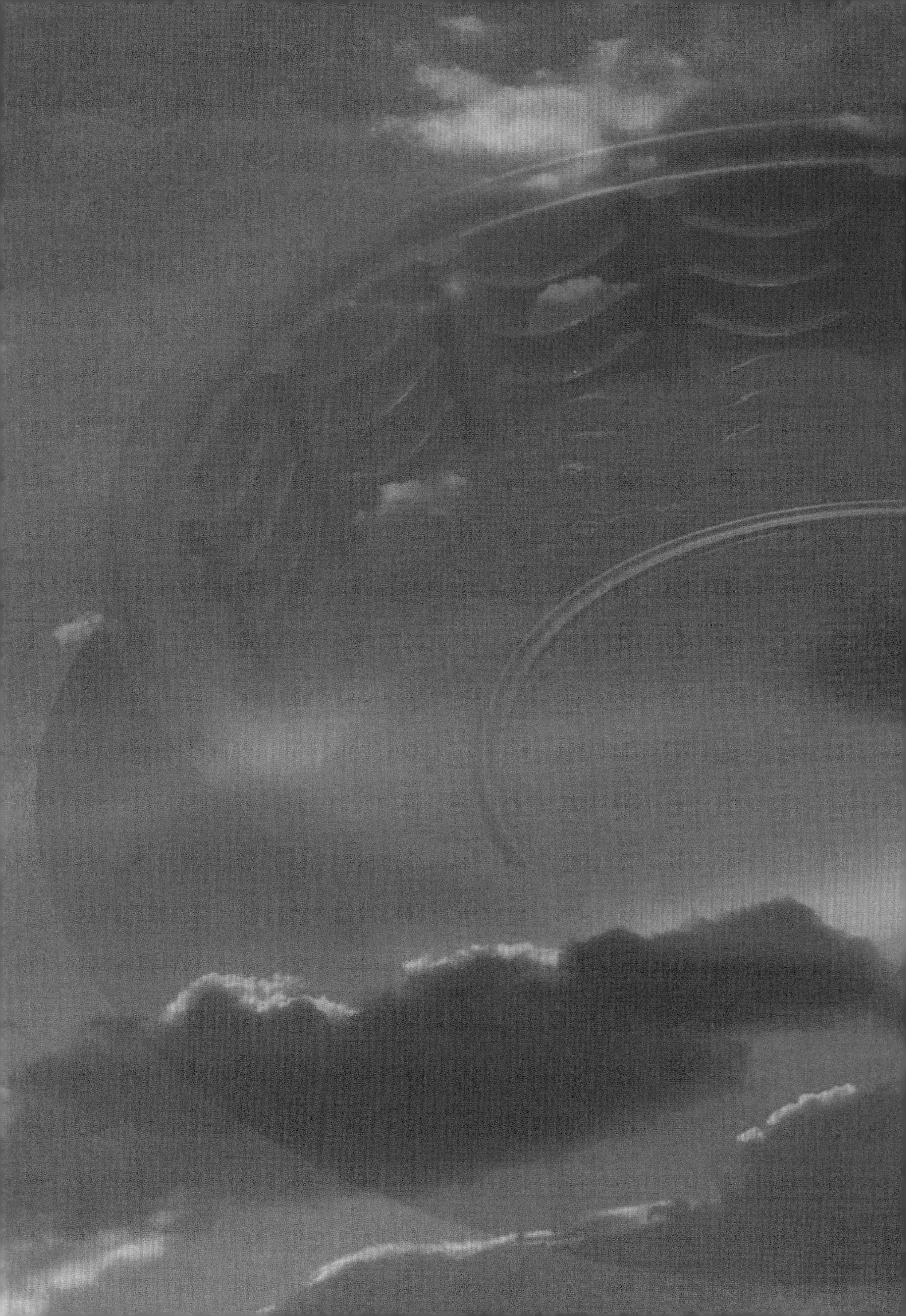

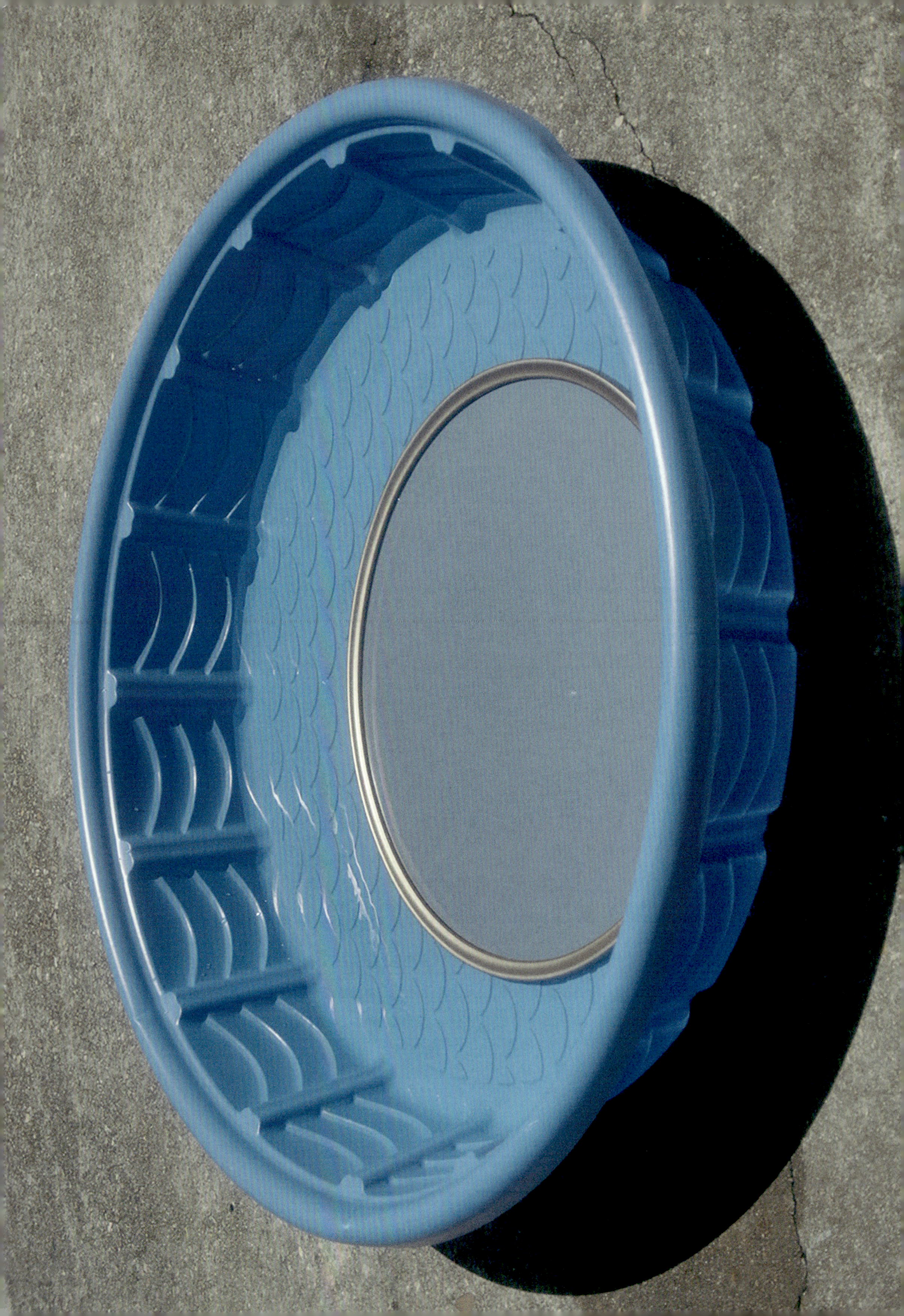

a Negro, a Lim-o

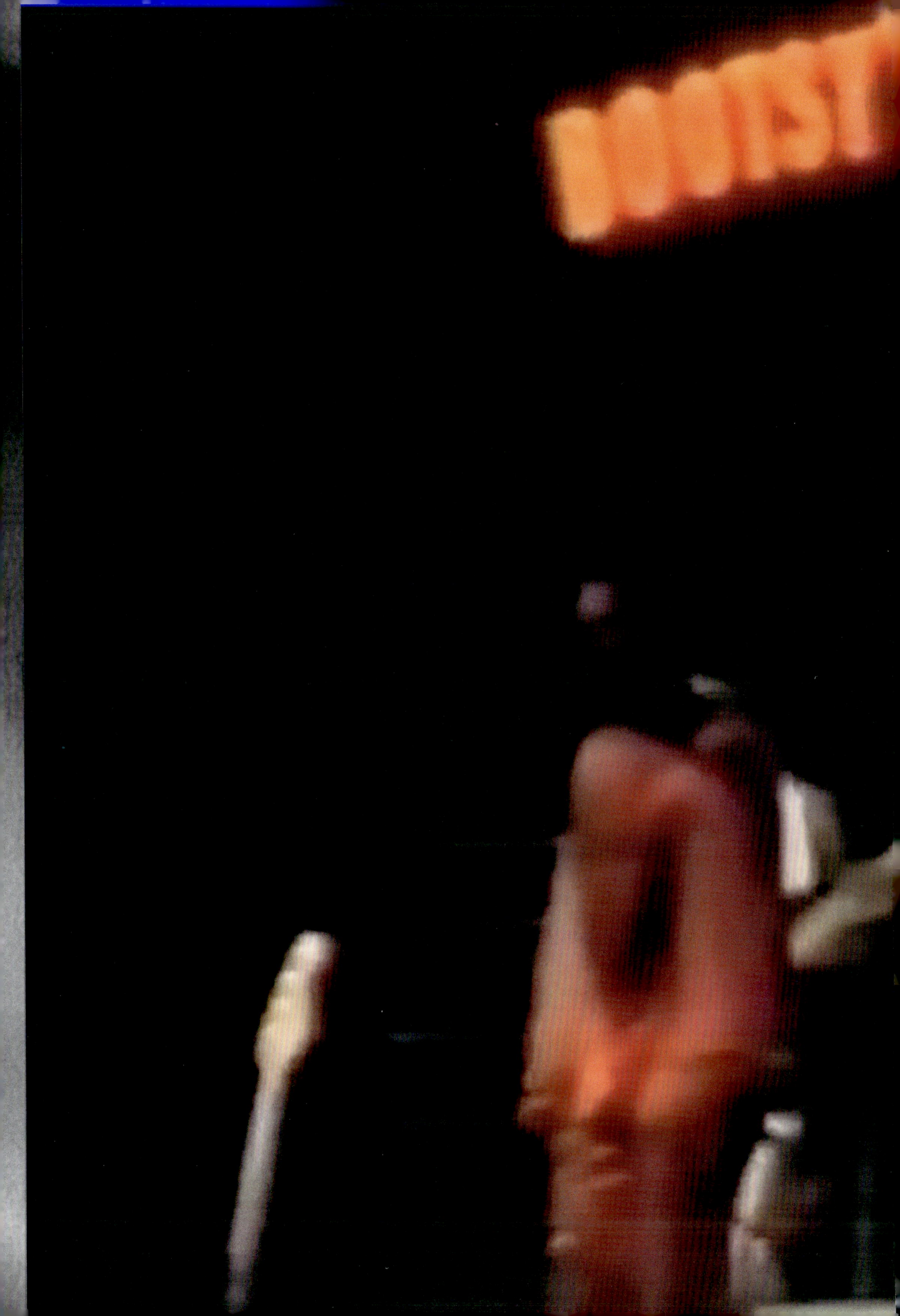

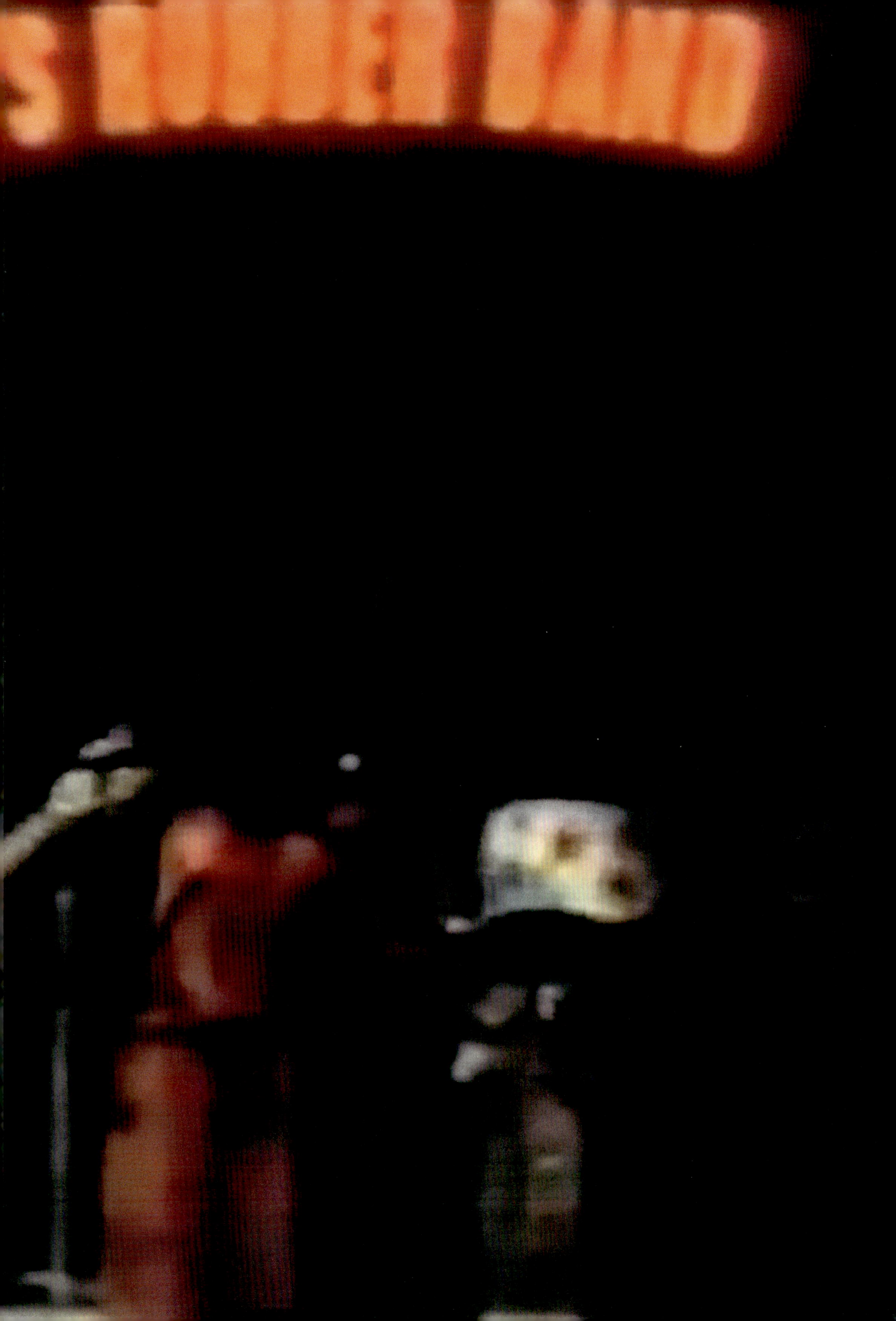

I don't
want to talk
about it

Let me just take my time

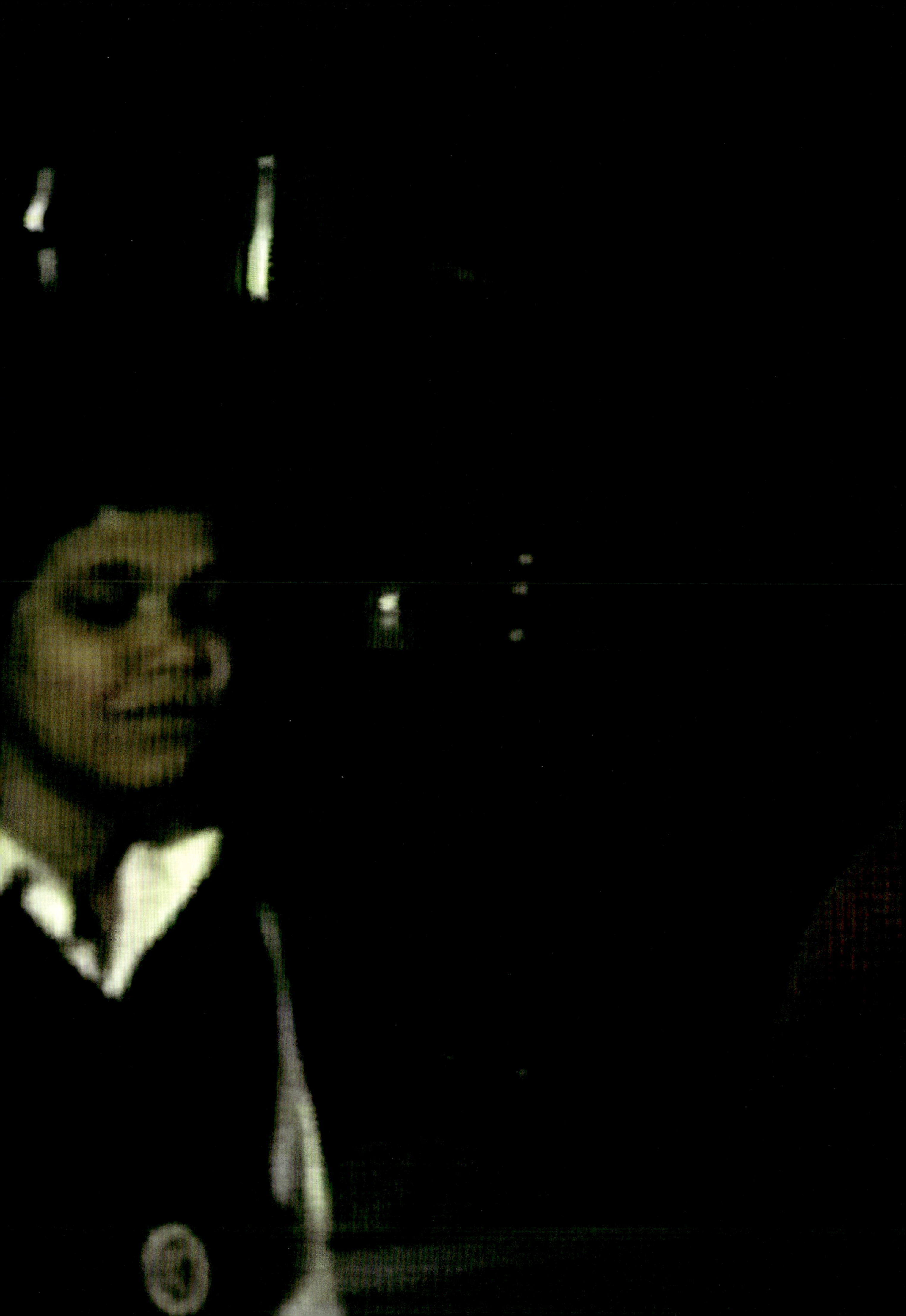

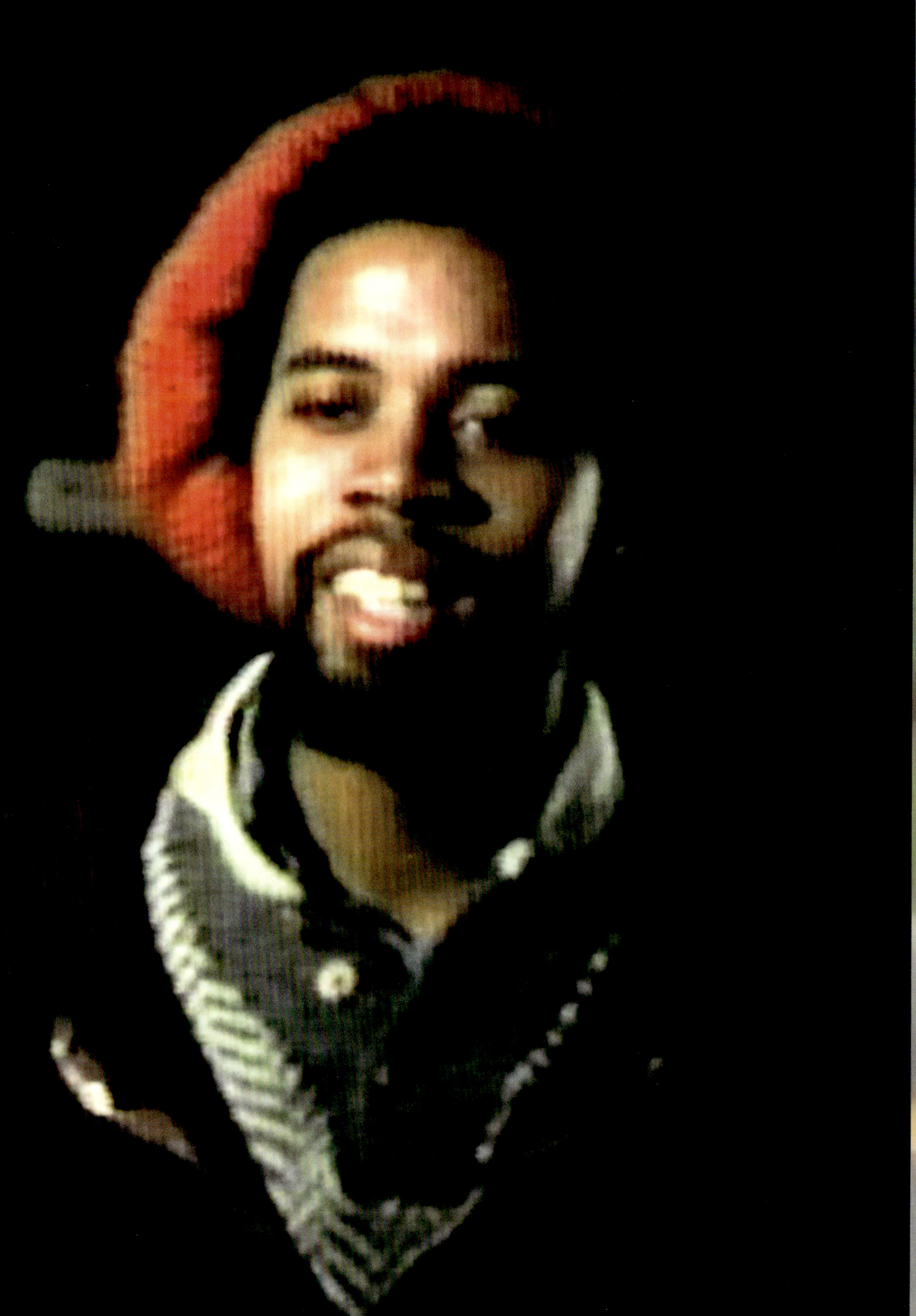

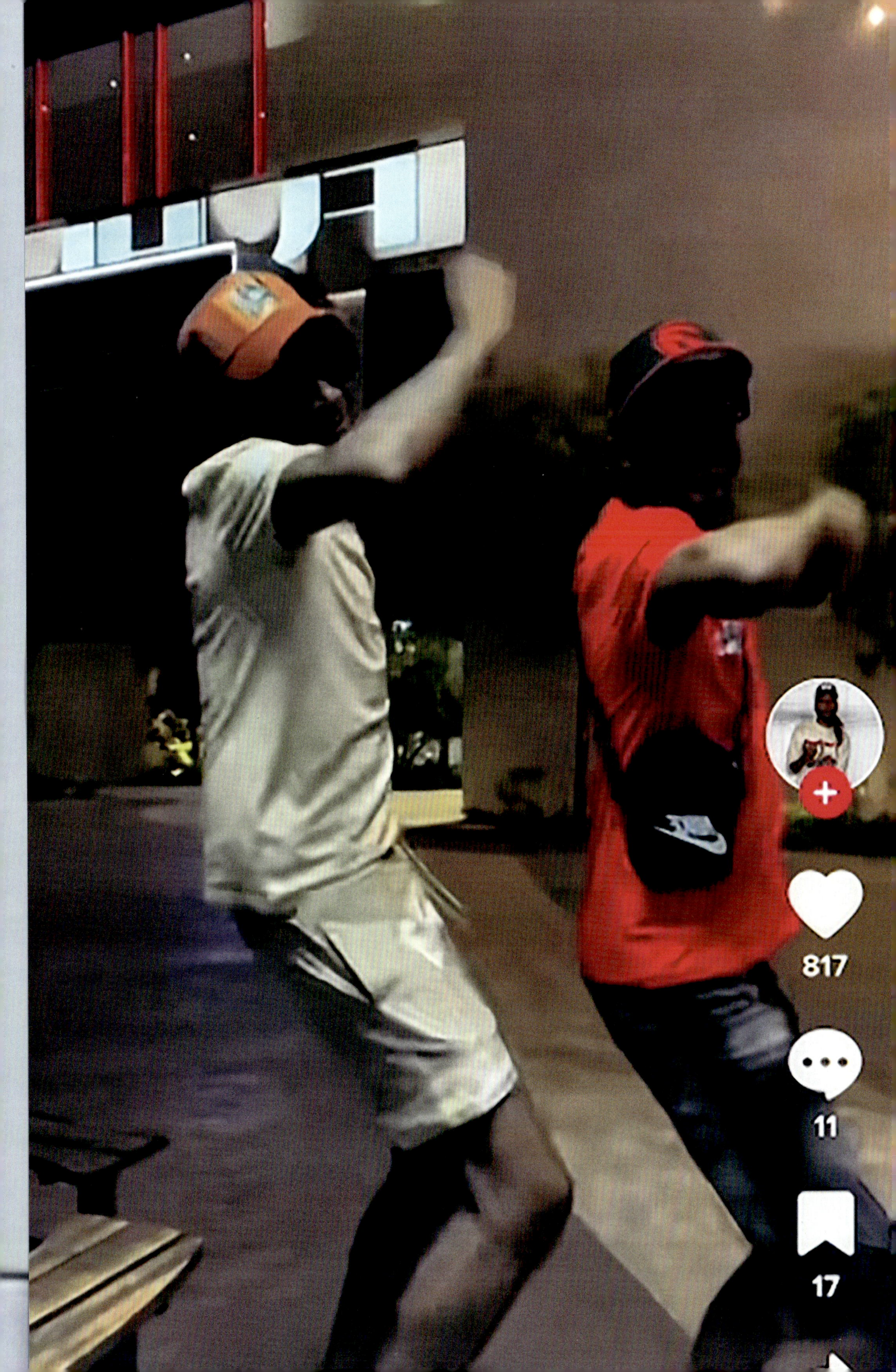
817
11
17

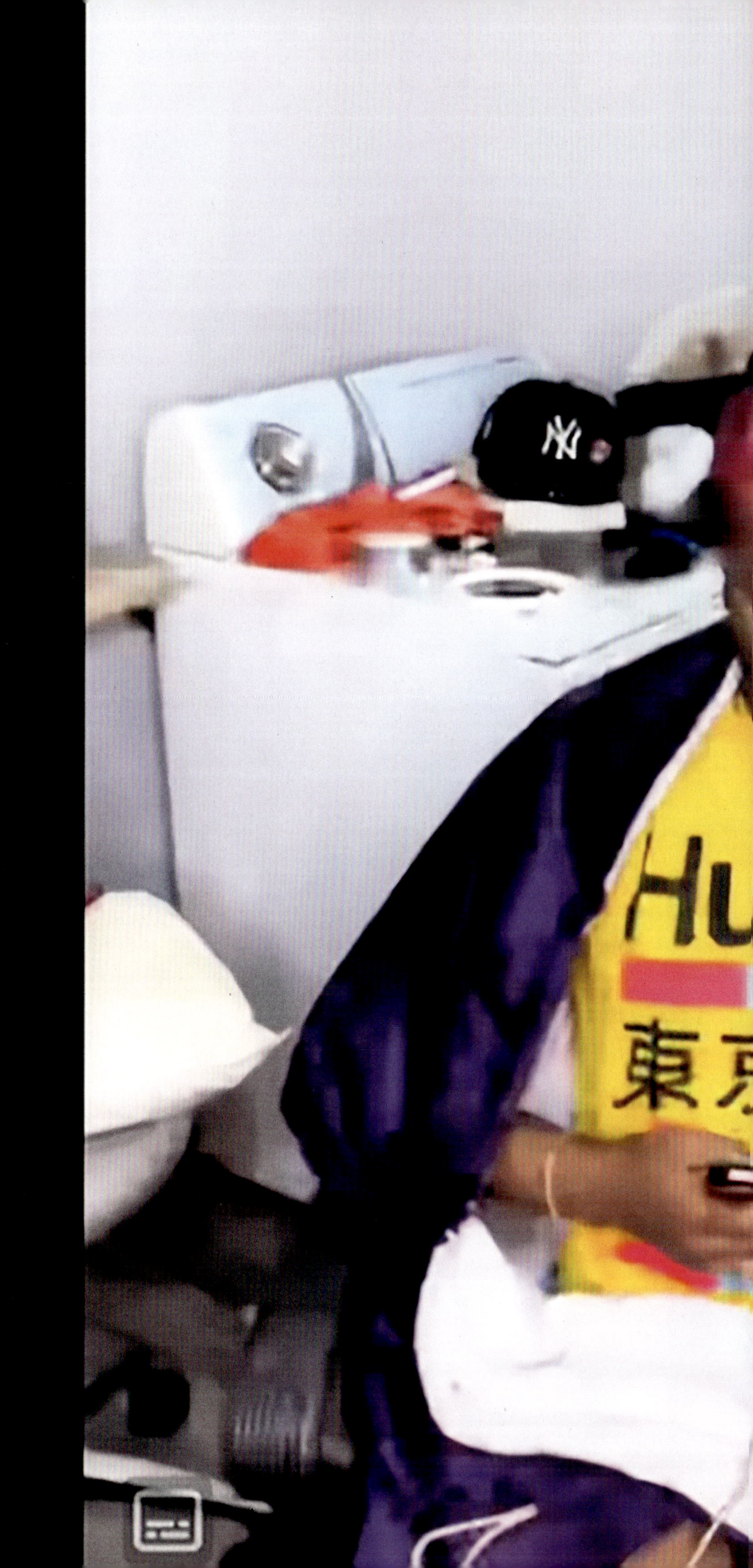
Hu
東京

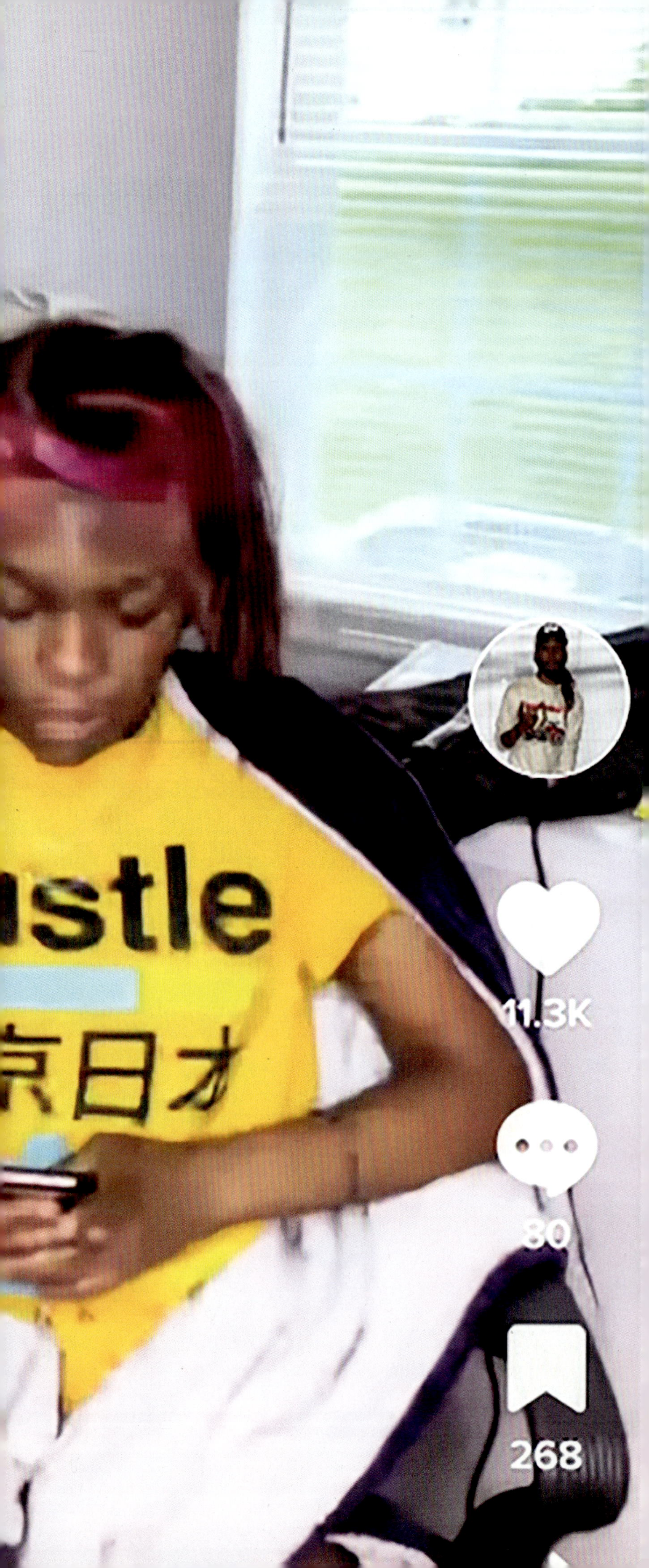

stle
東日才
11.3K
80
268

I'd rather
be with you

How do you all feel out there?

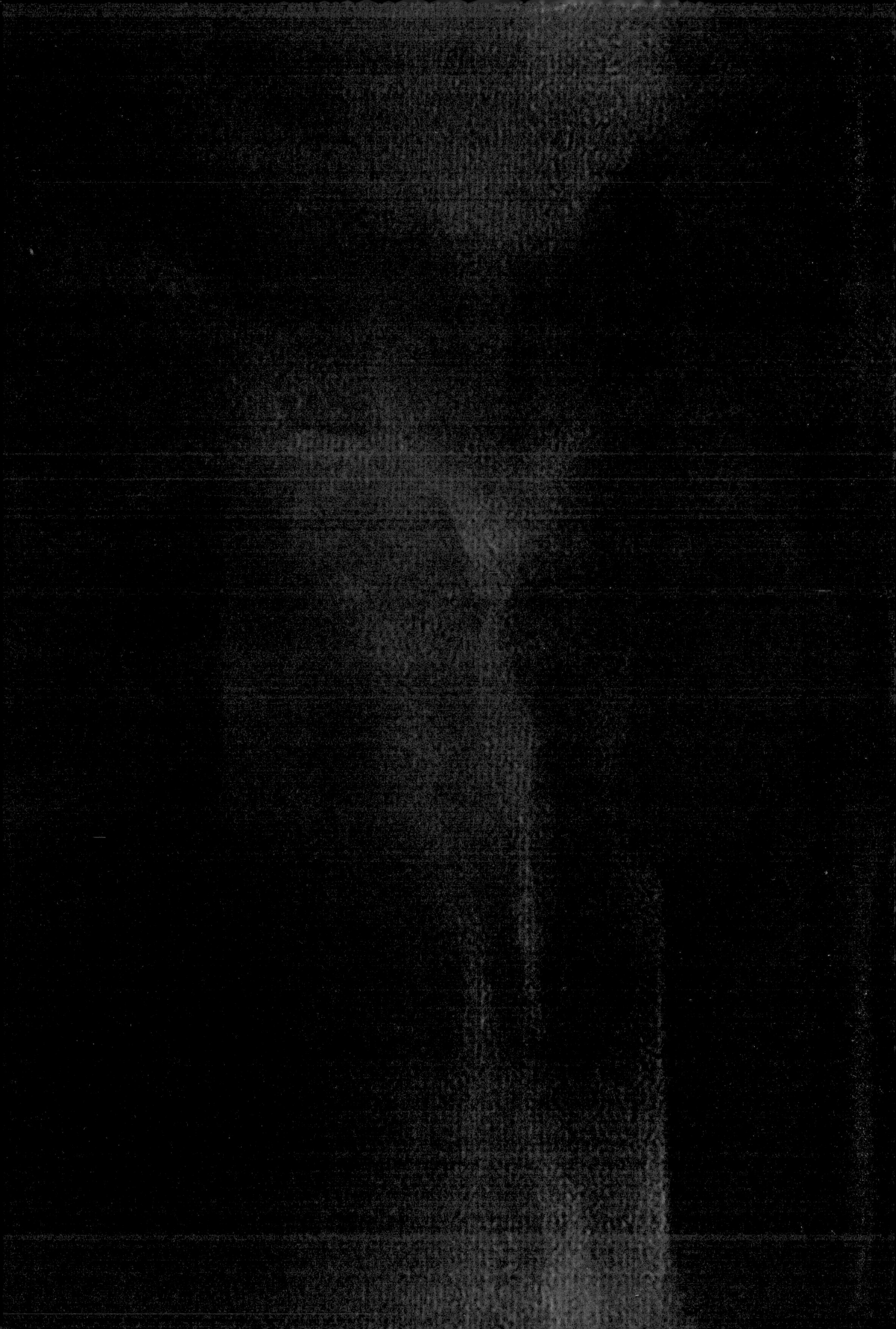

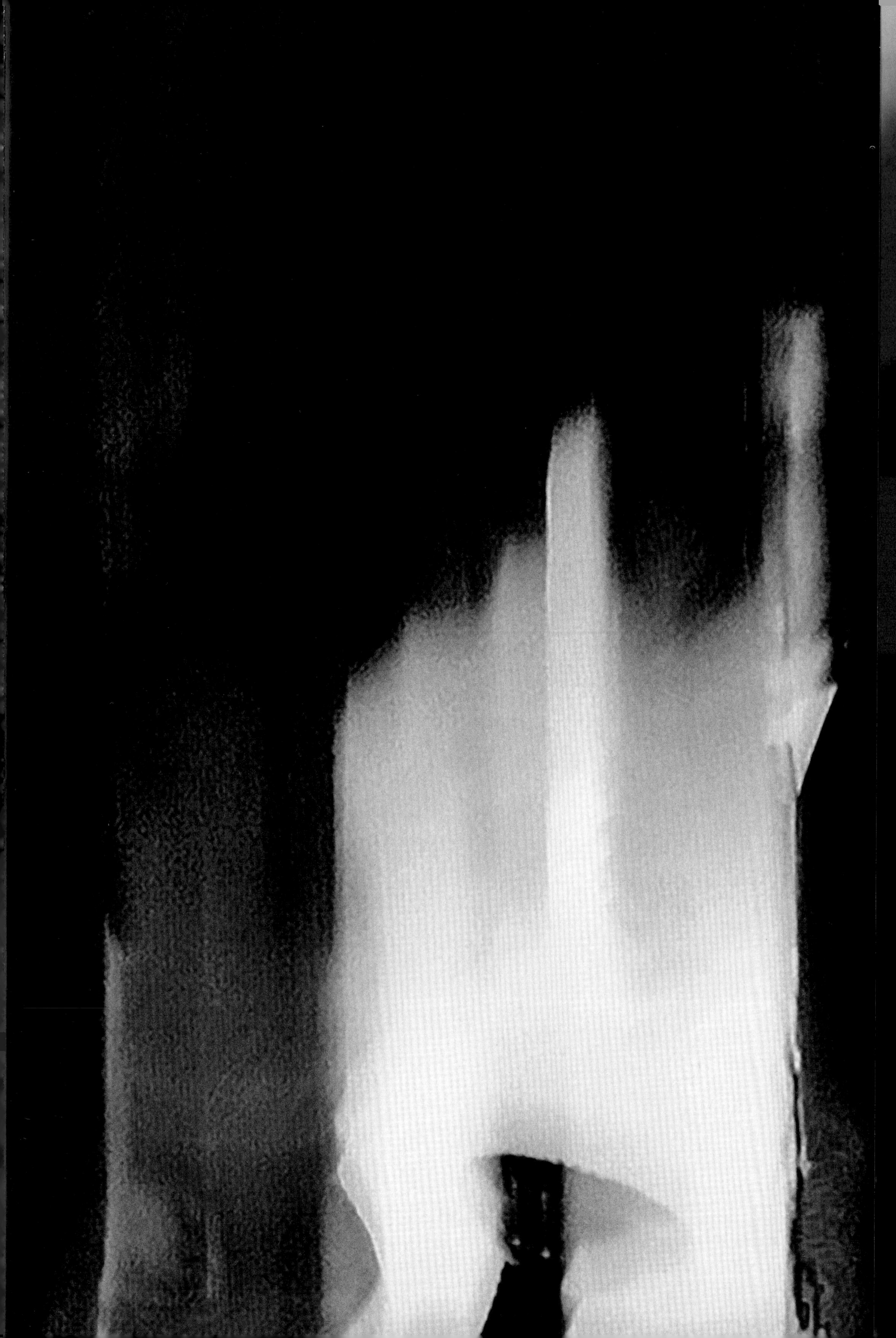

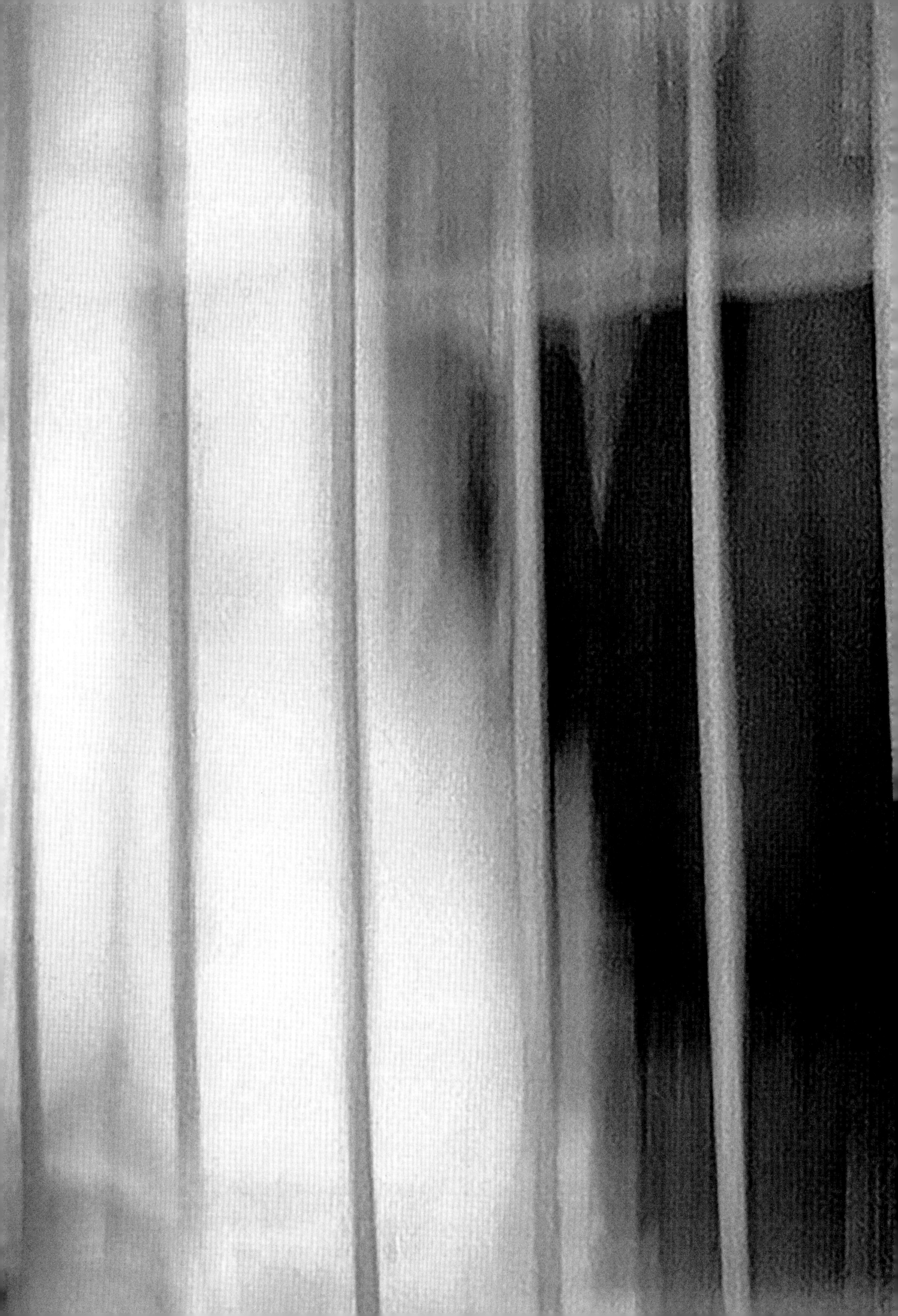

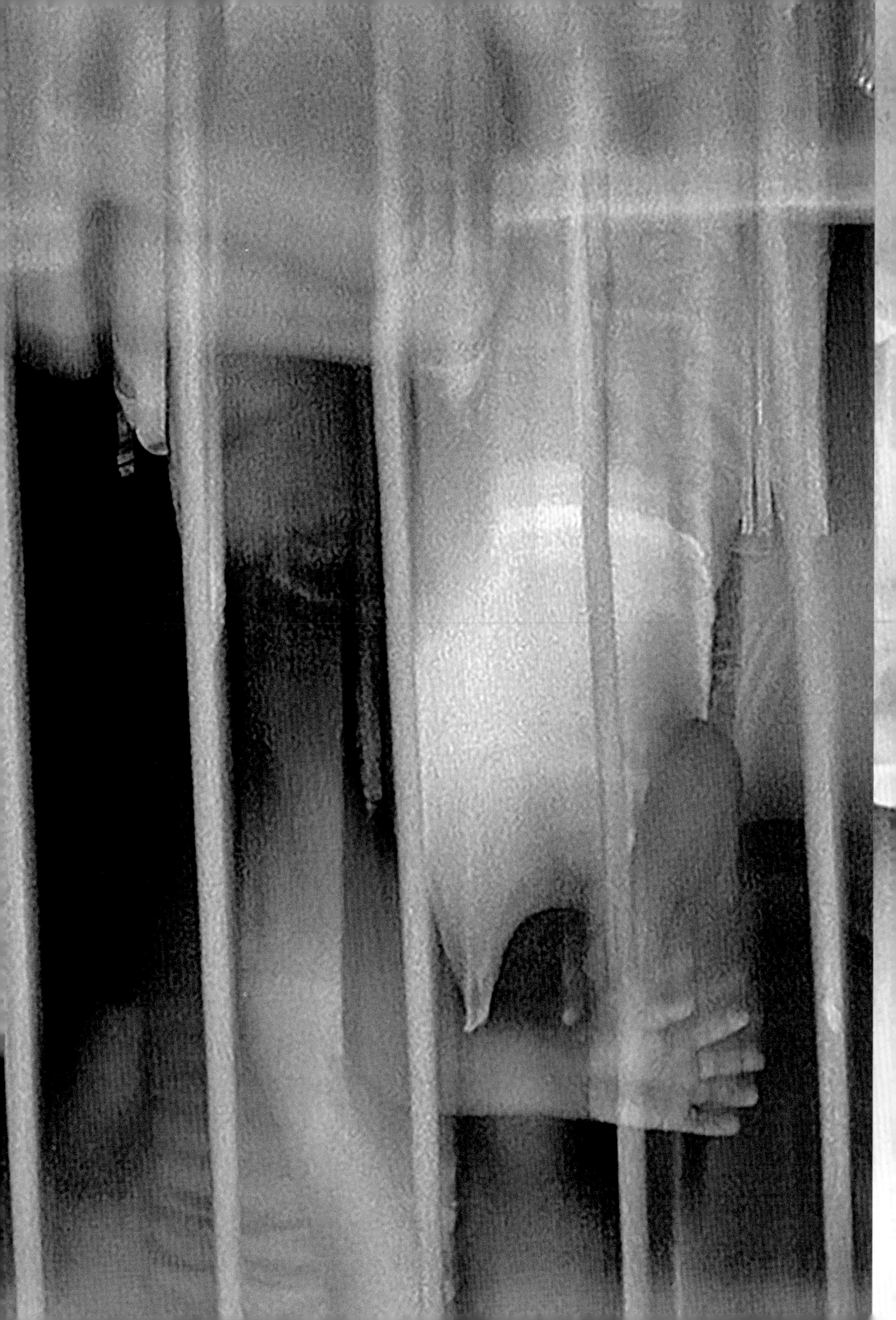

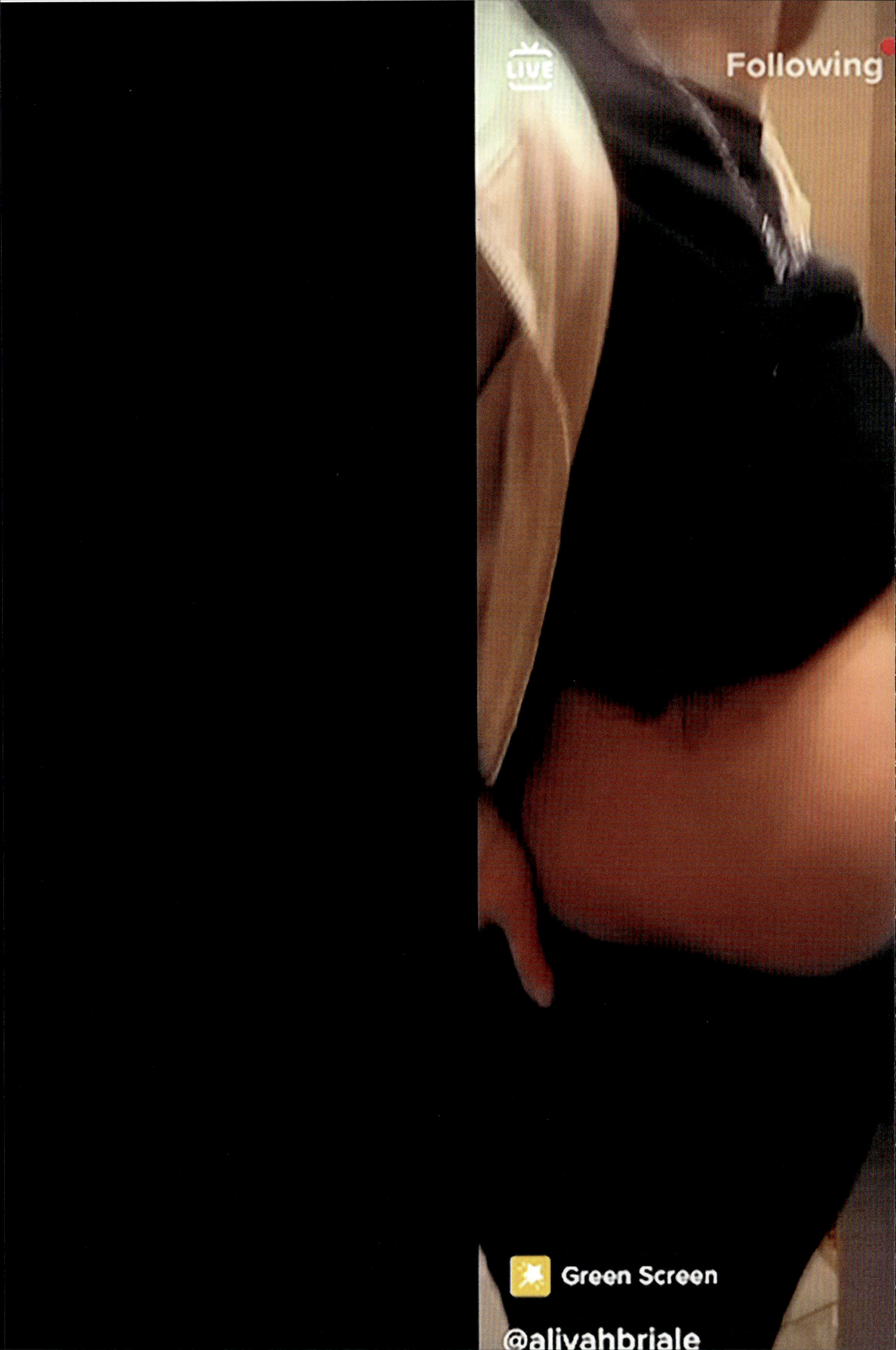

LIVE
Following
Green Screen
@aliyahbriale

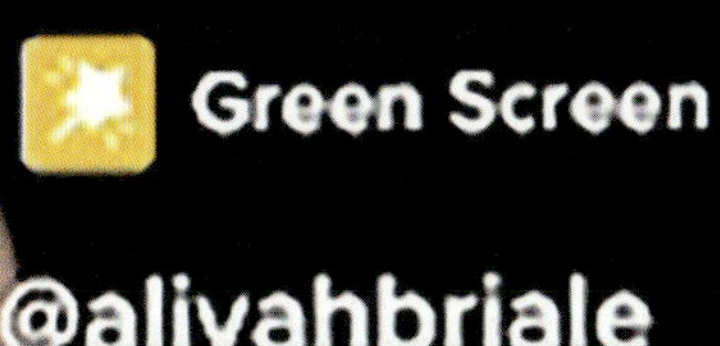

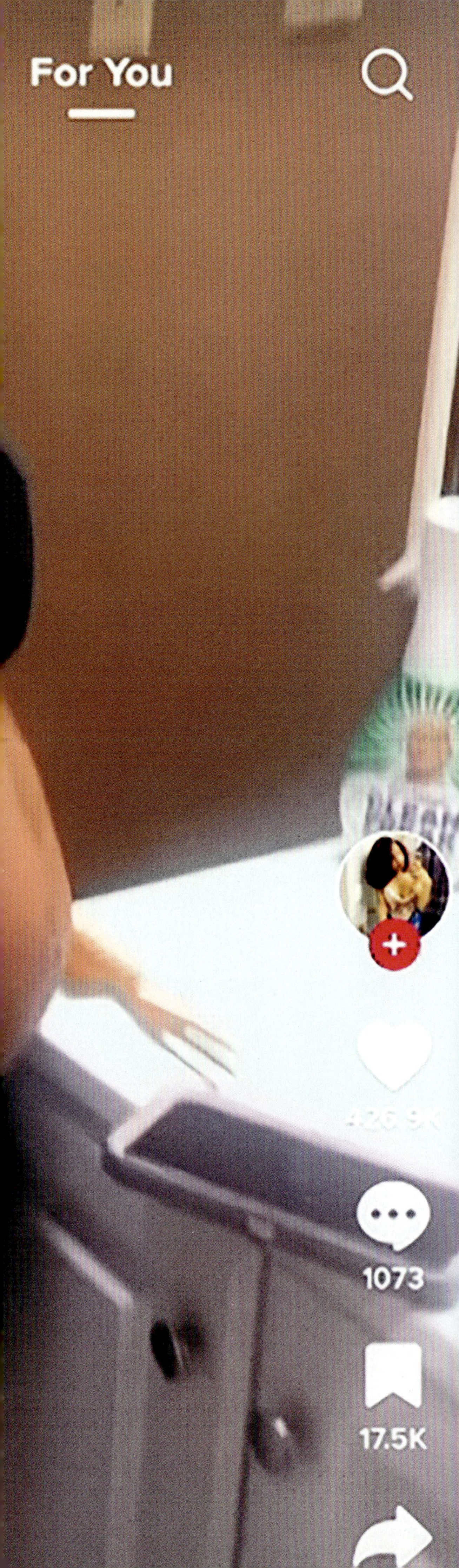
For You
17.5K
1073
17.5K

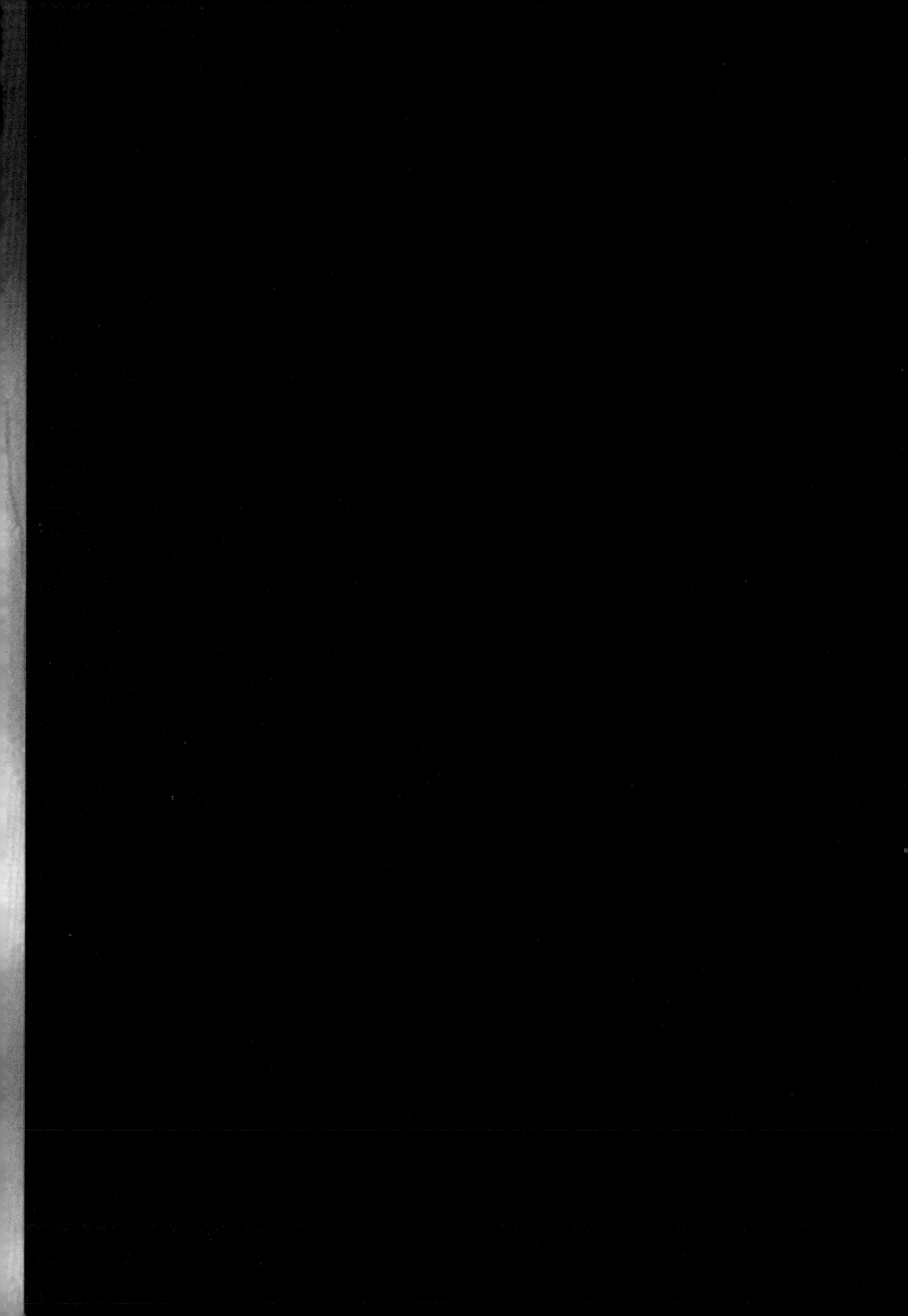

Safe

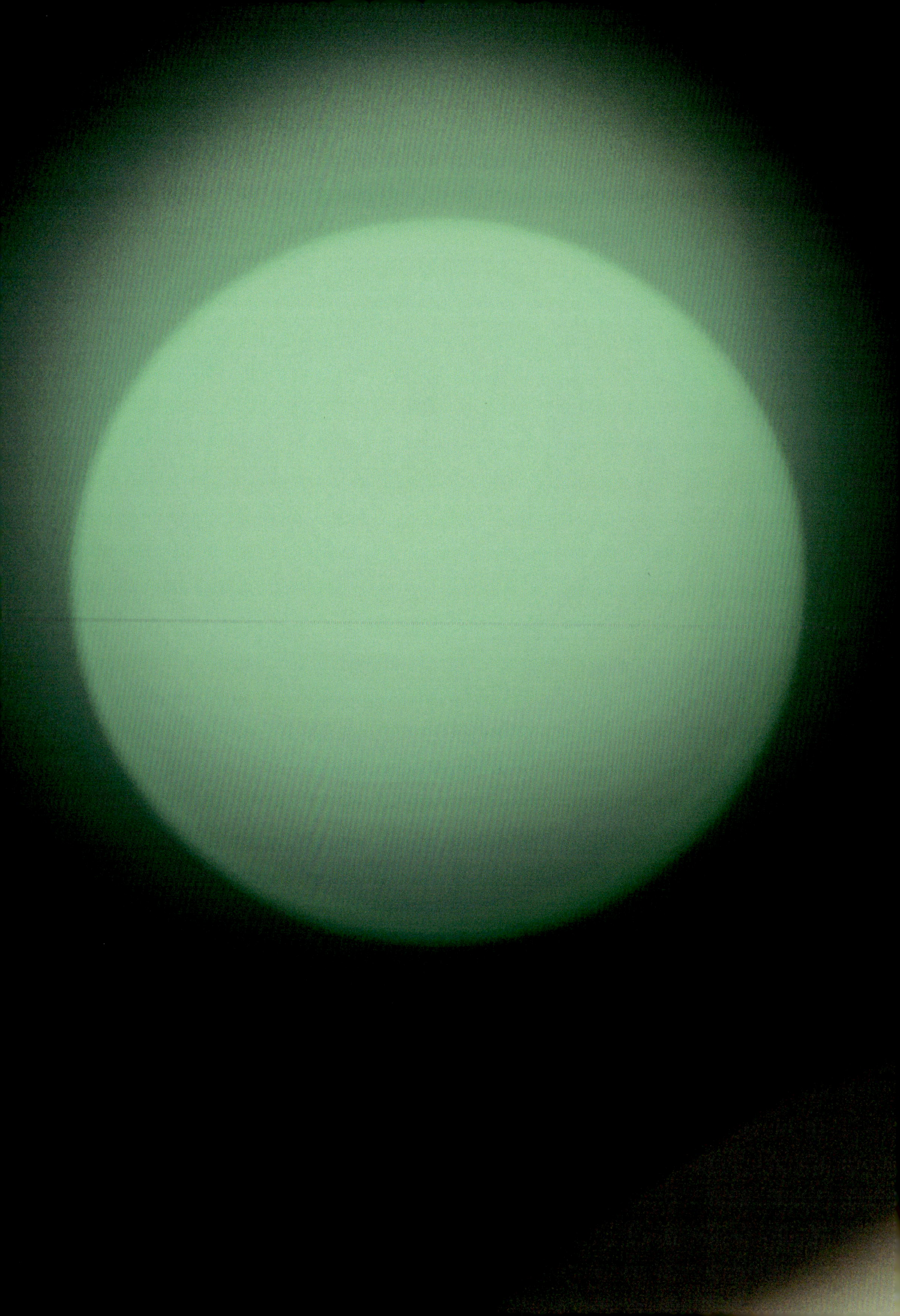

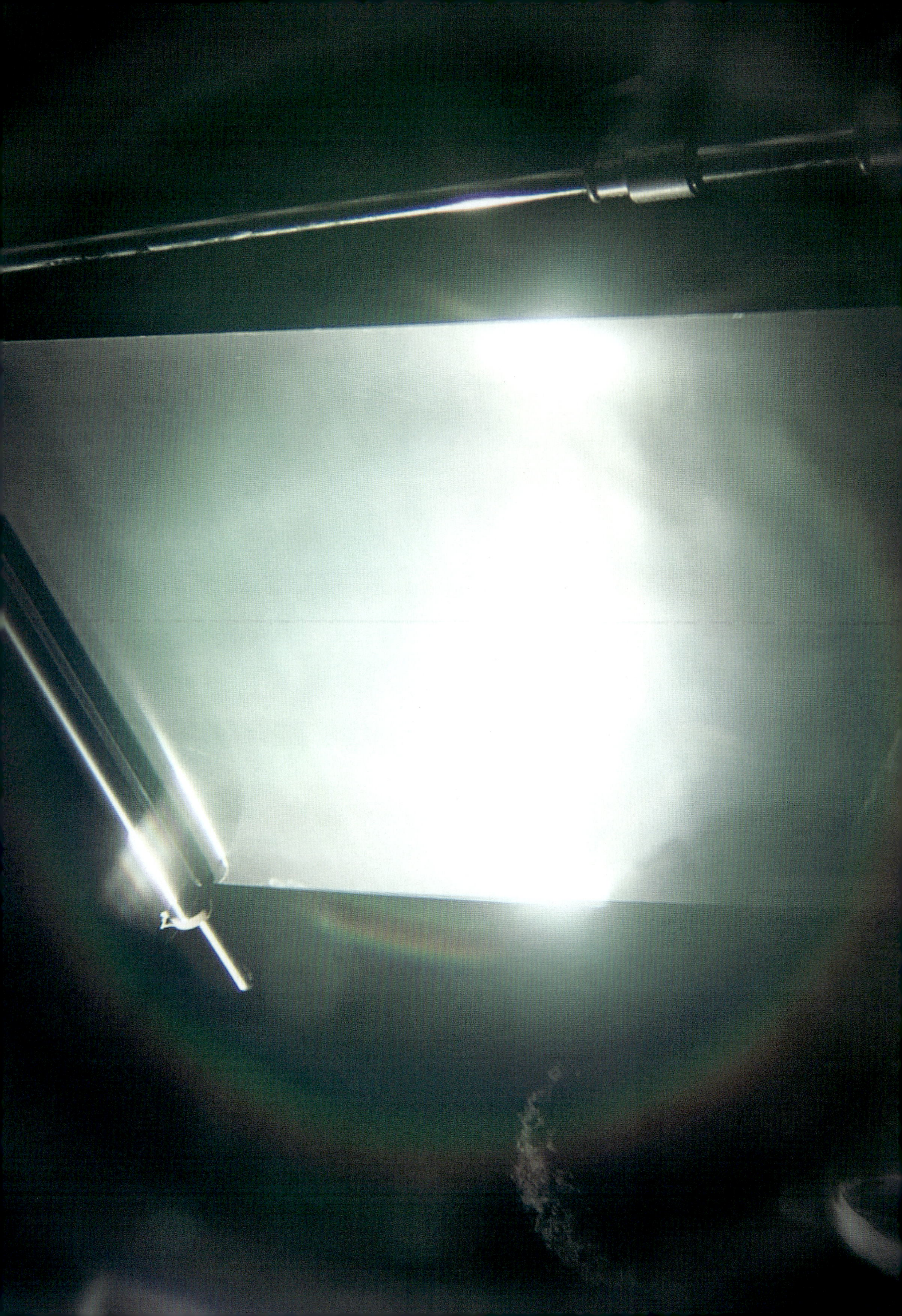

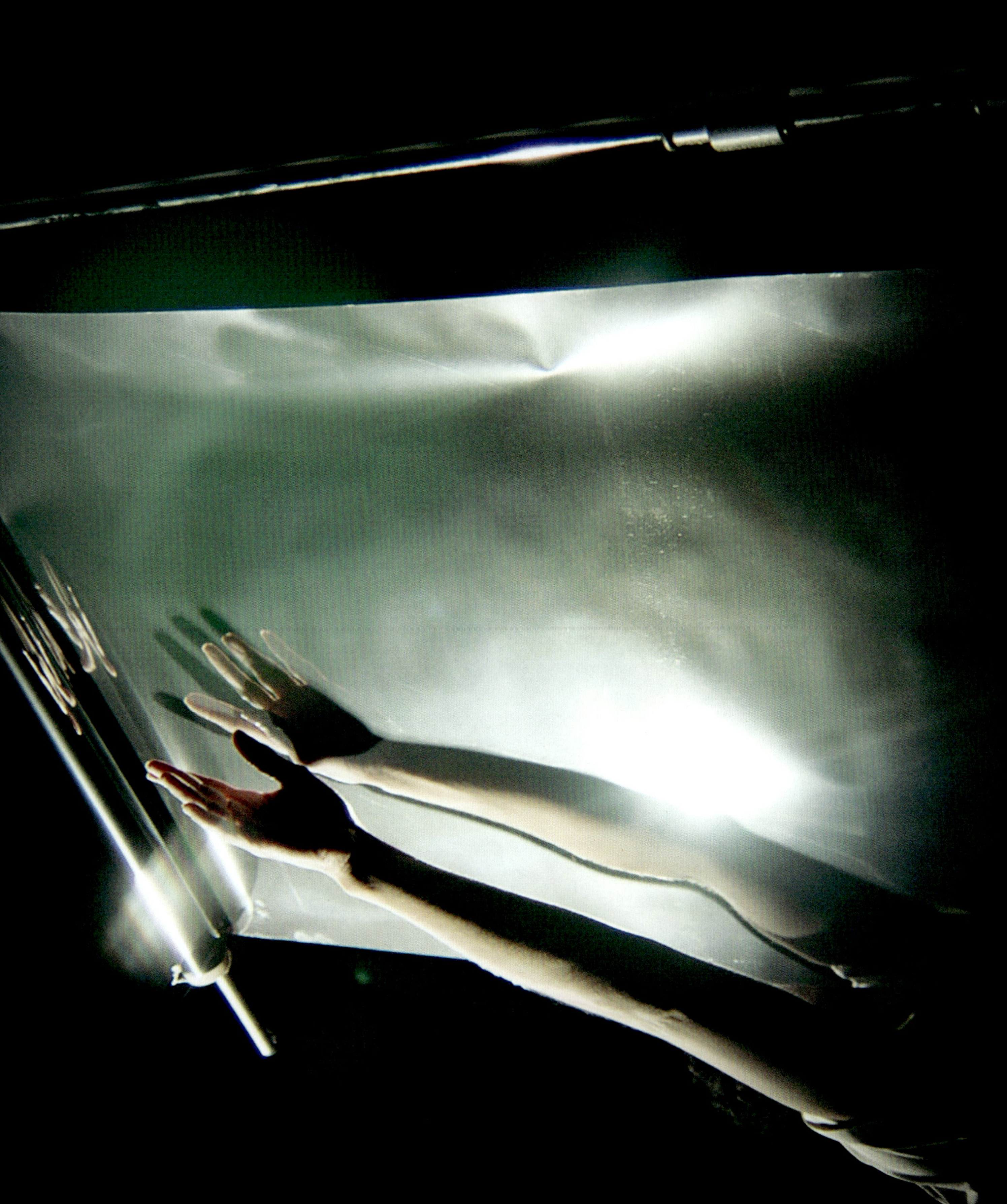

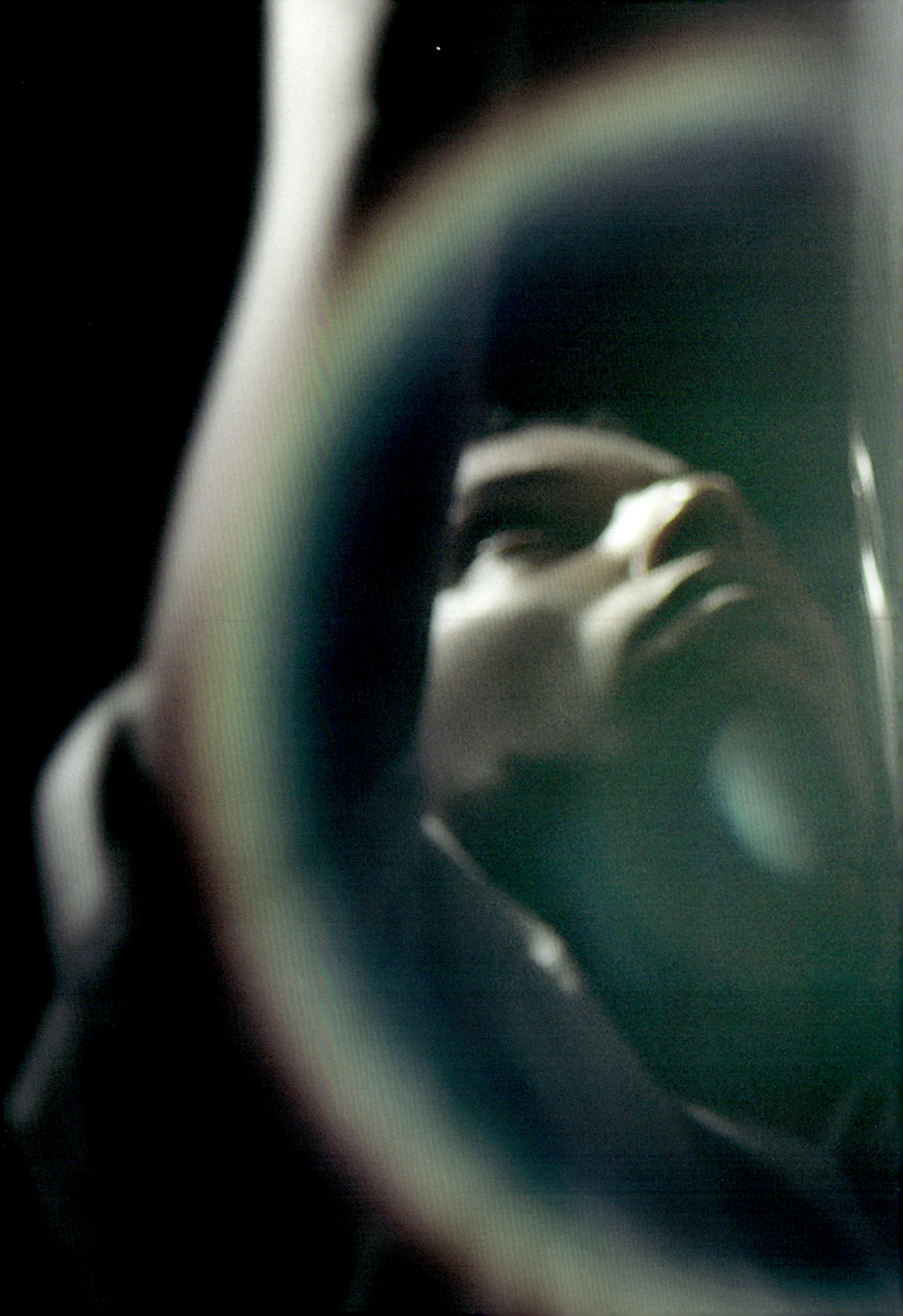

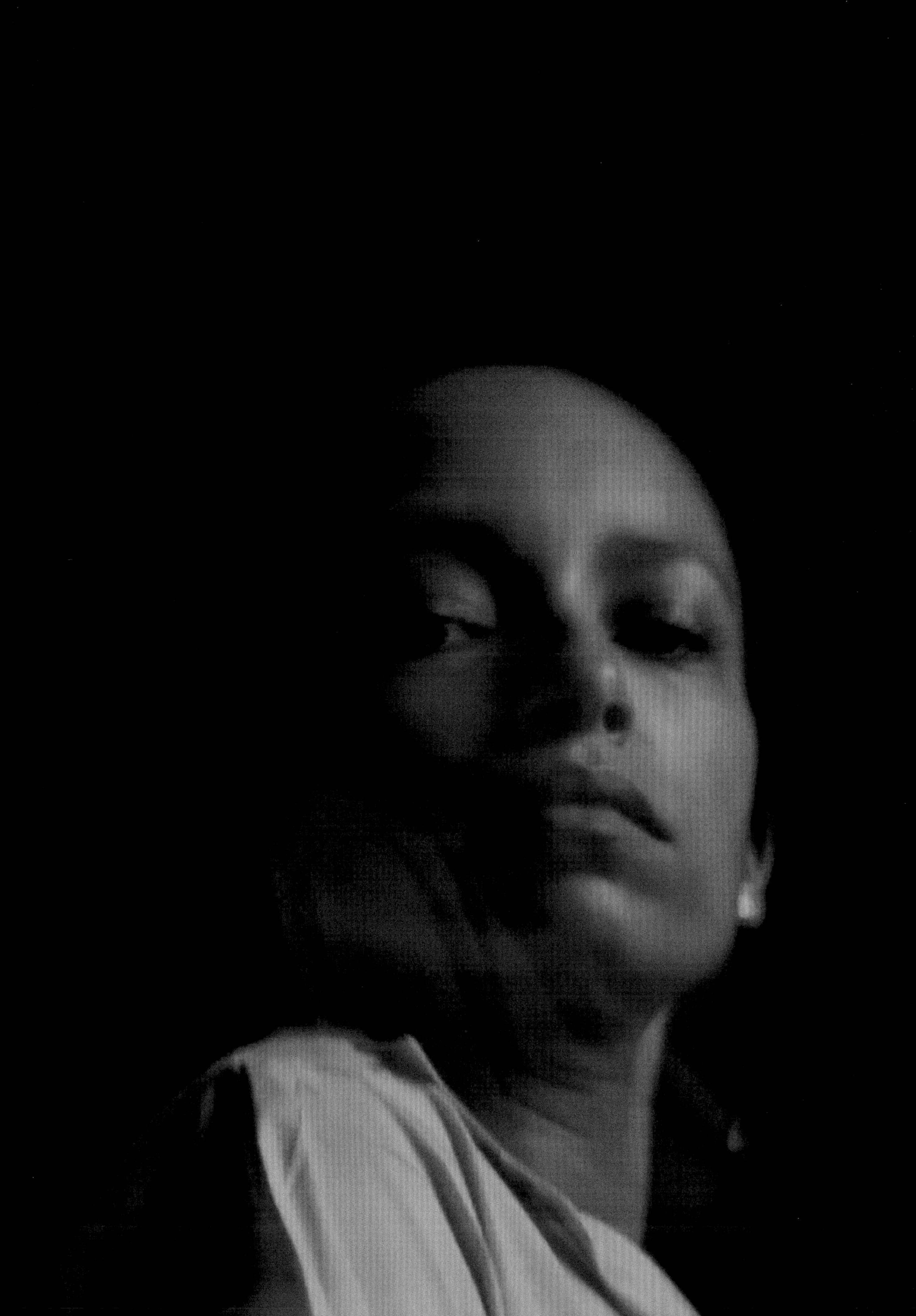

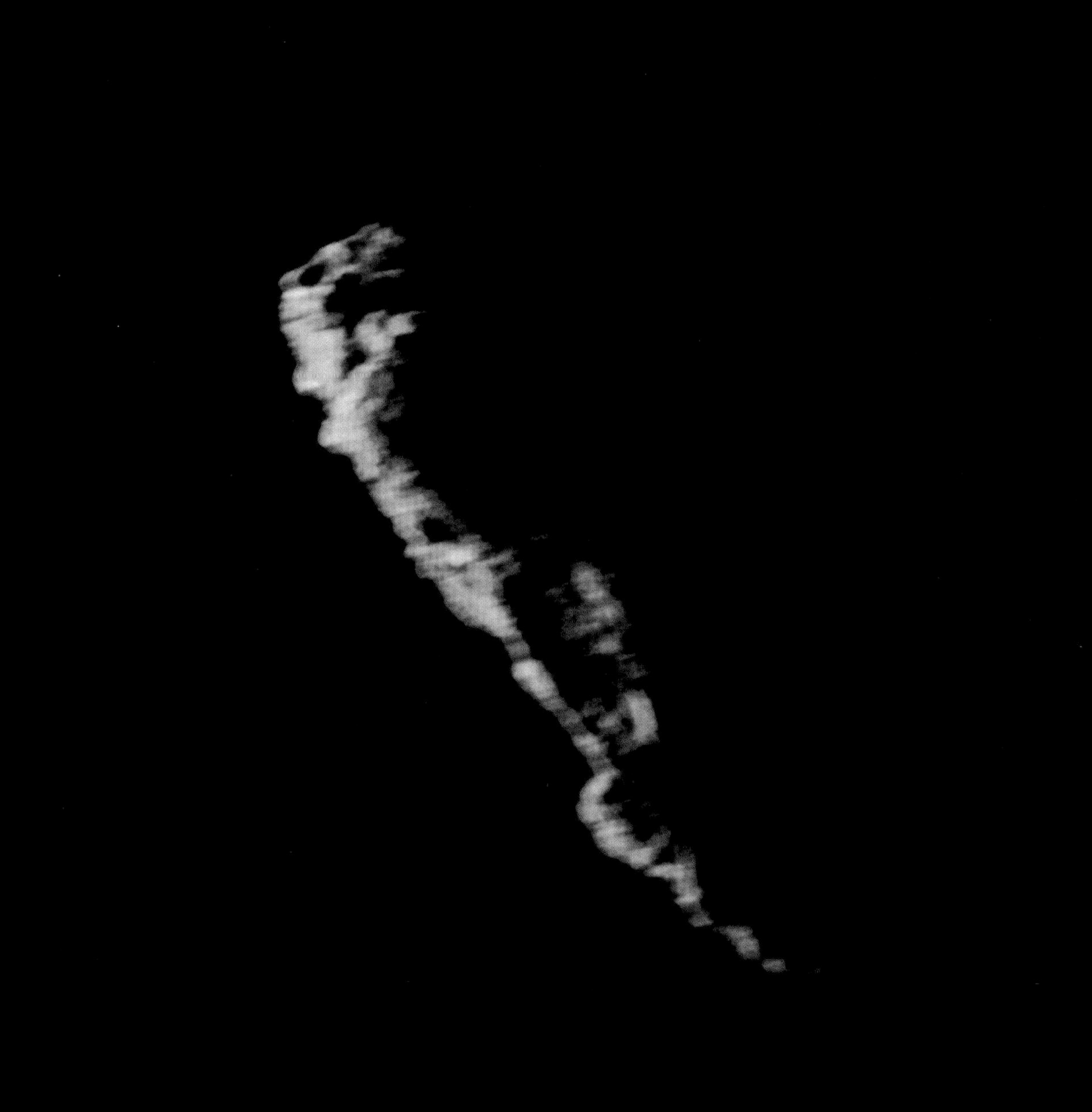

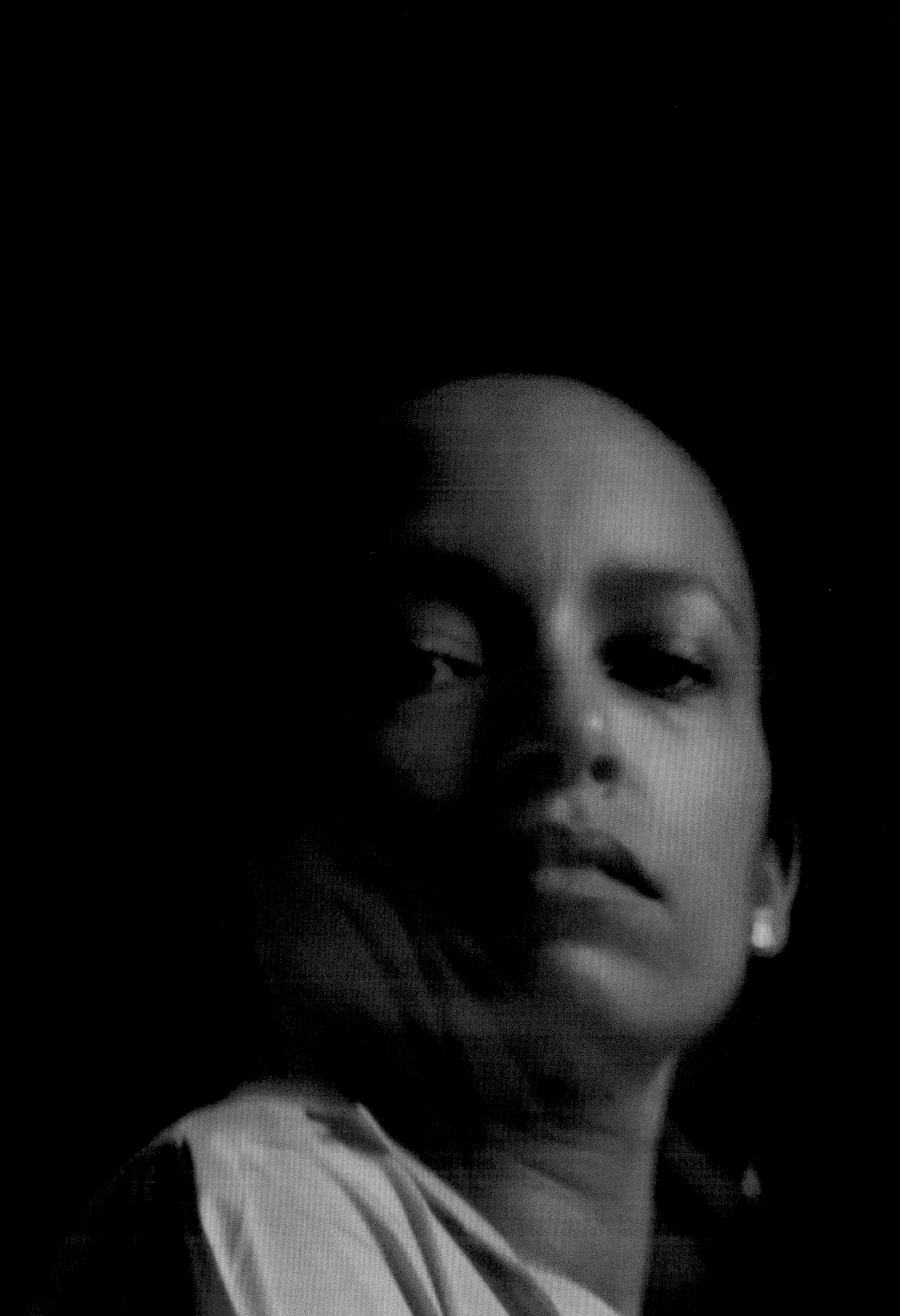

Anything you want

You can take them all

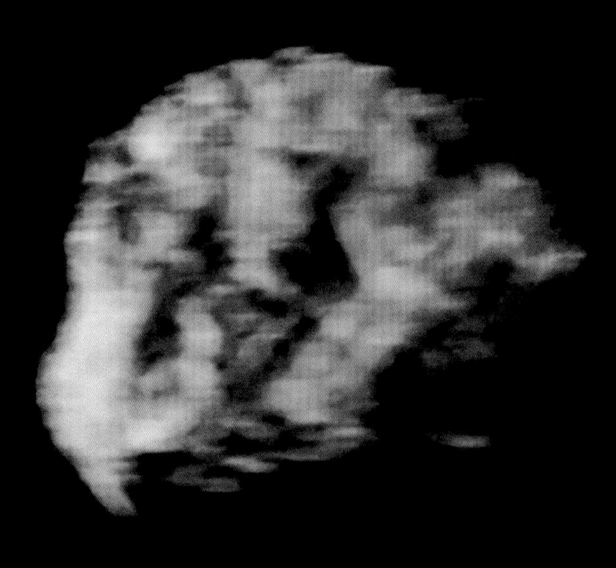

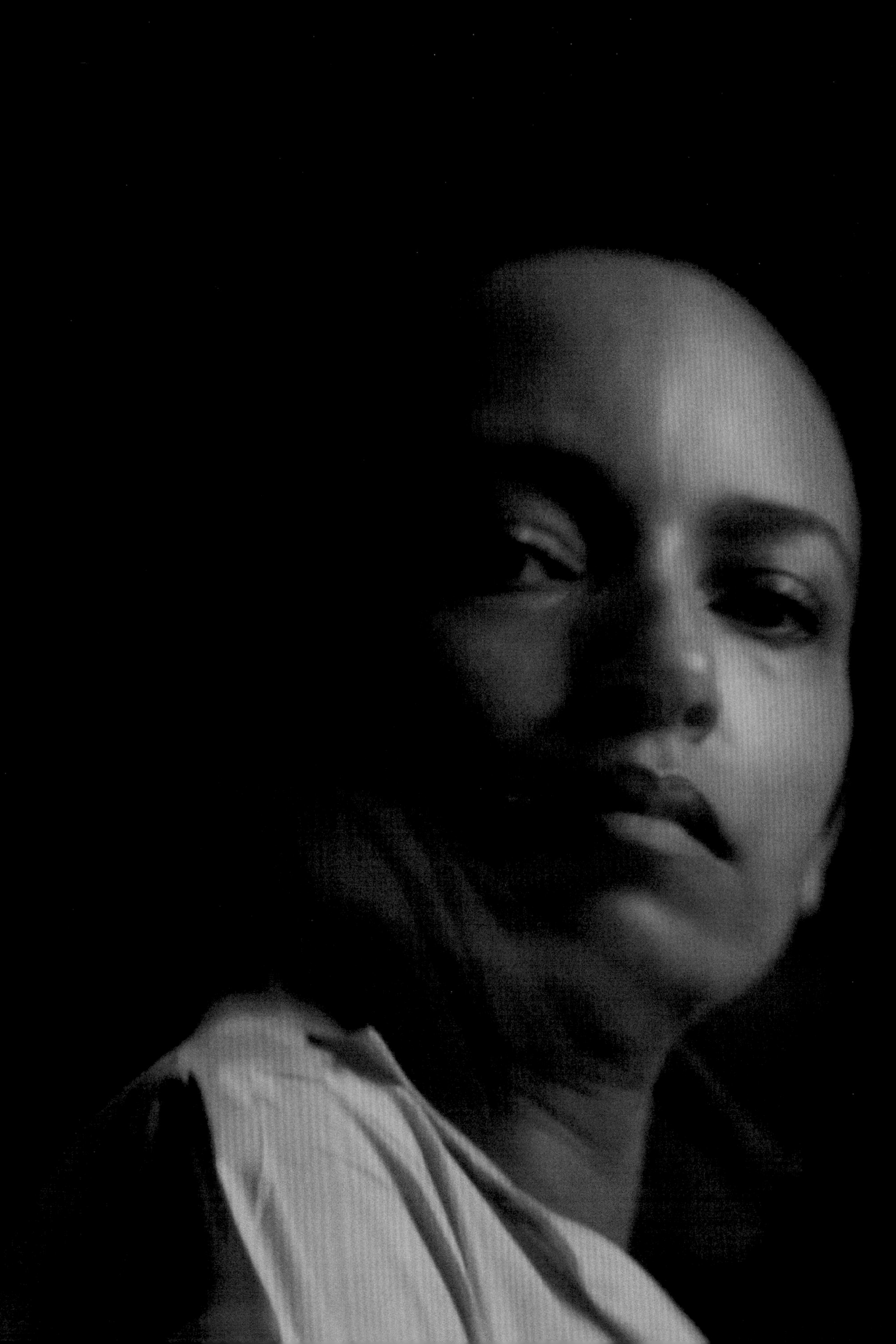

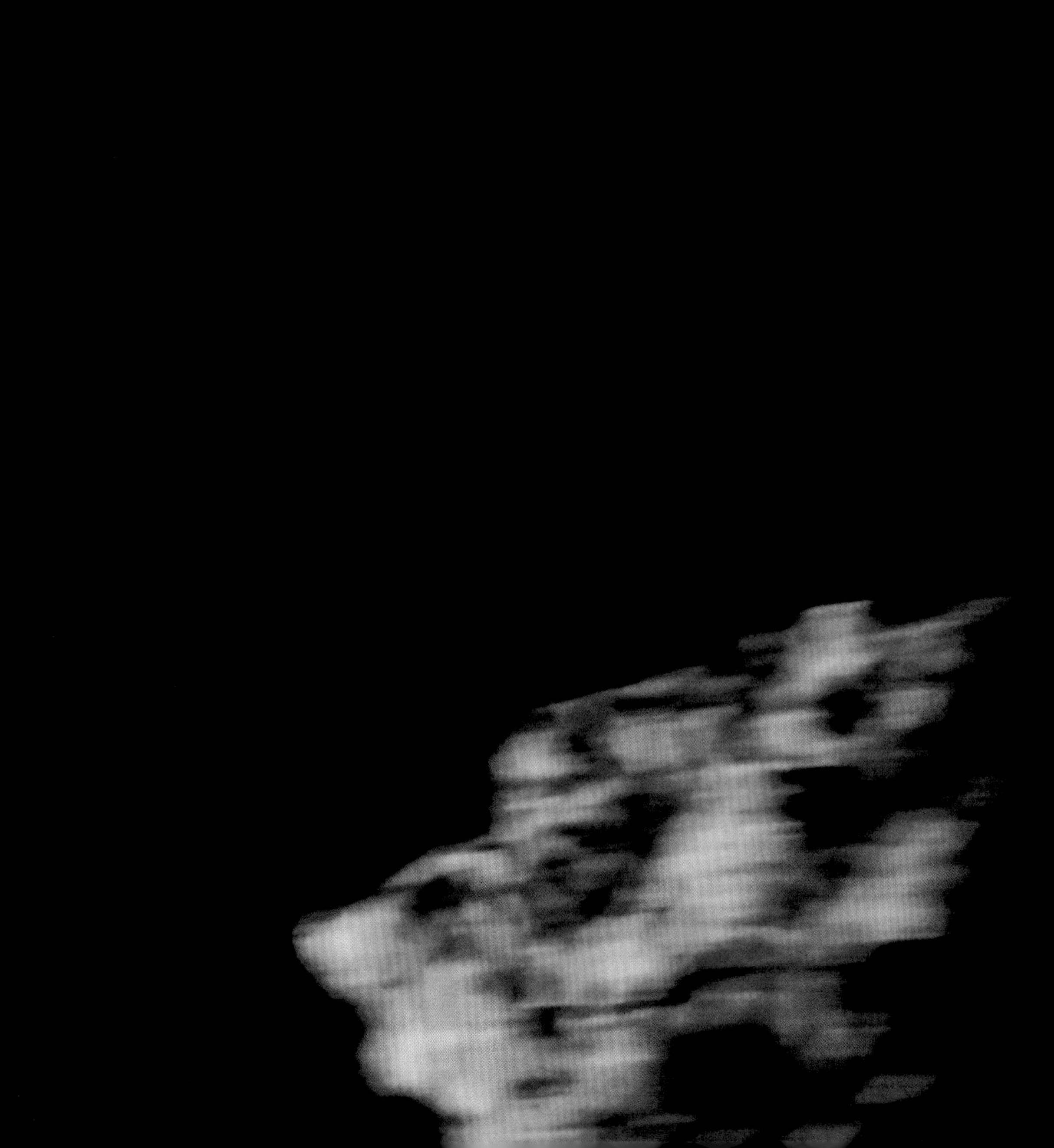

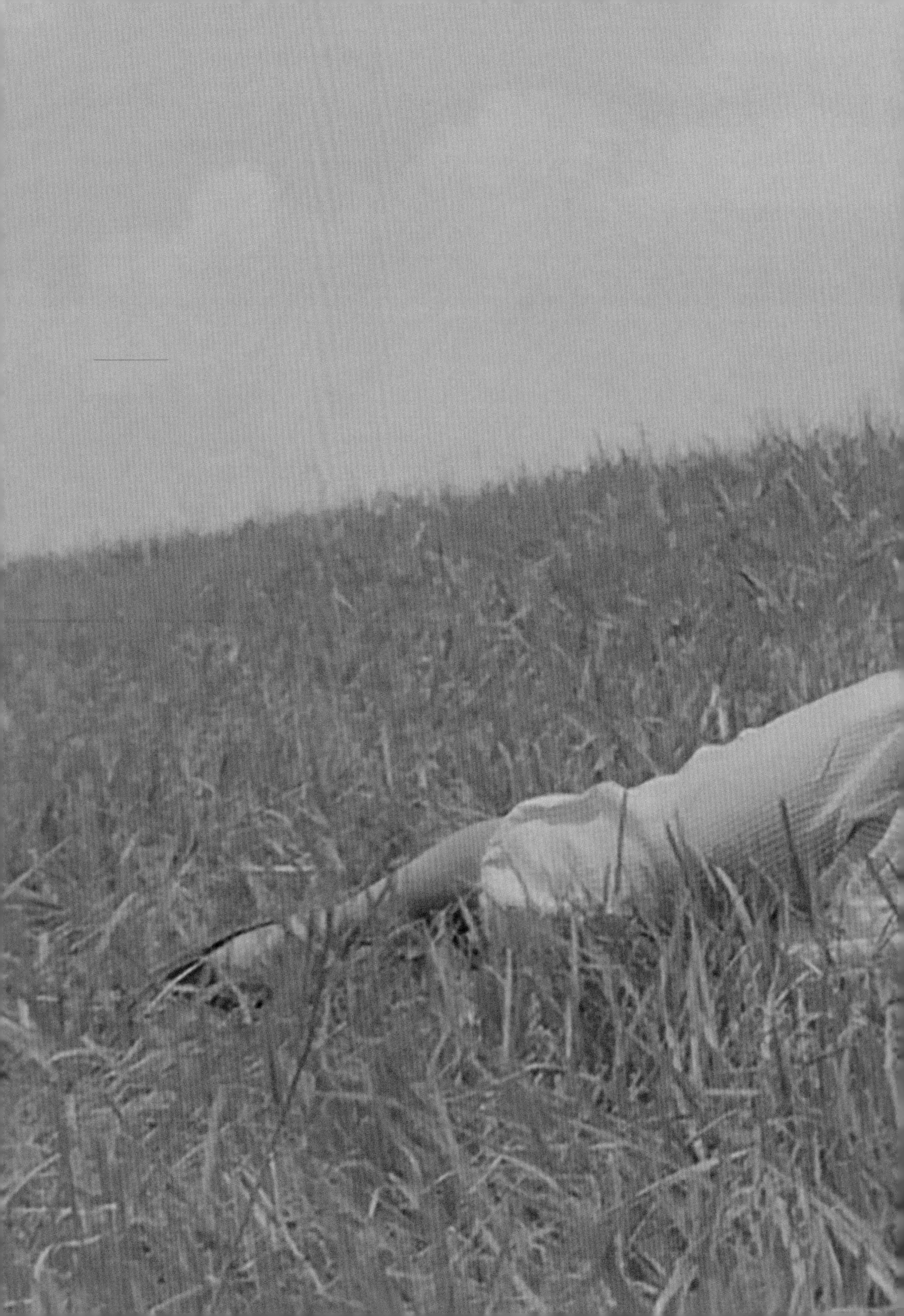

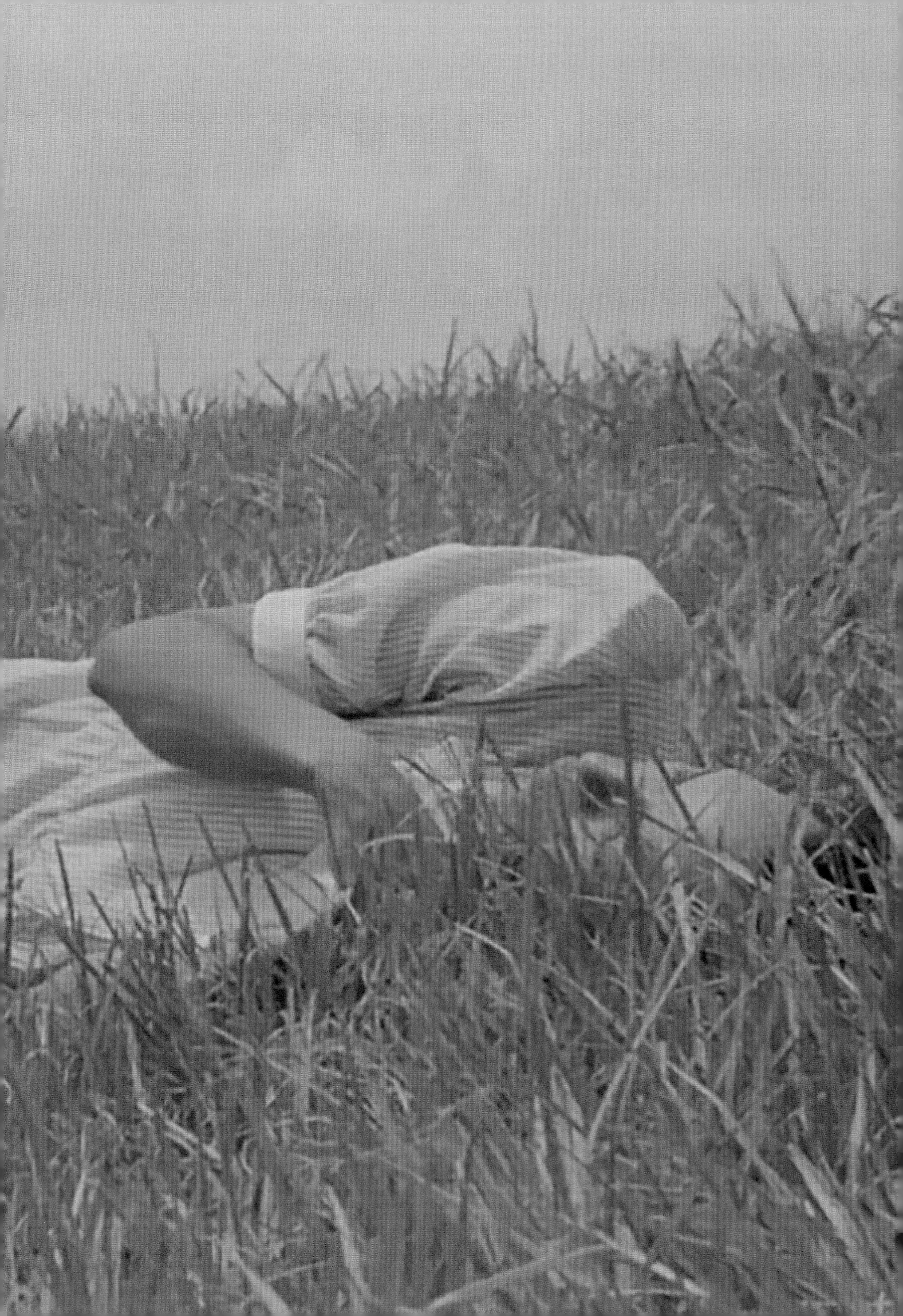

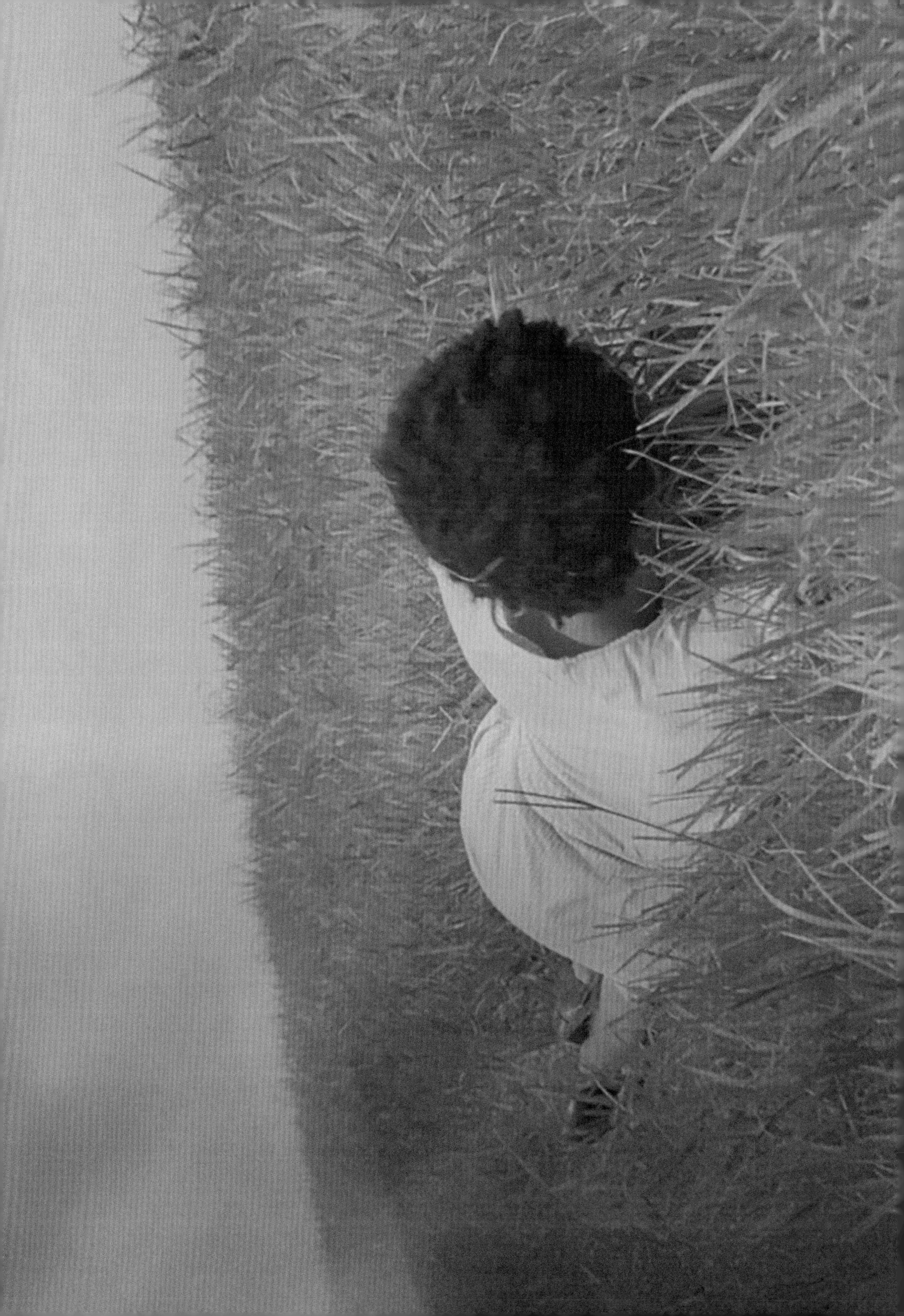

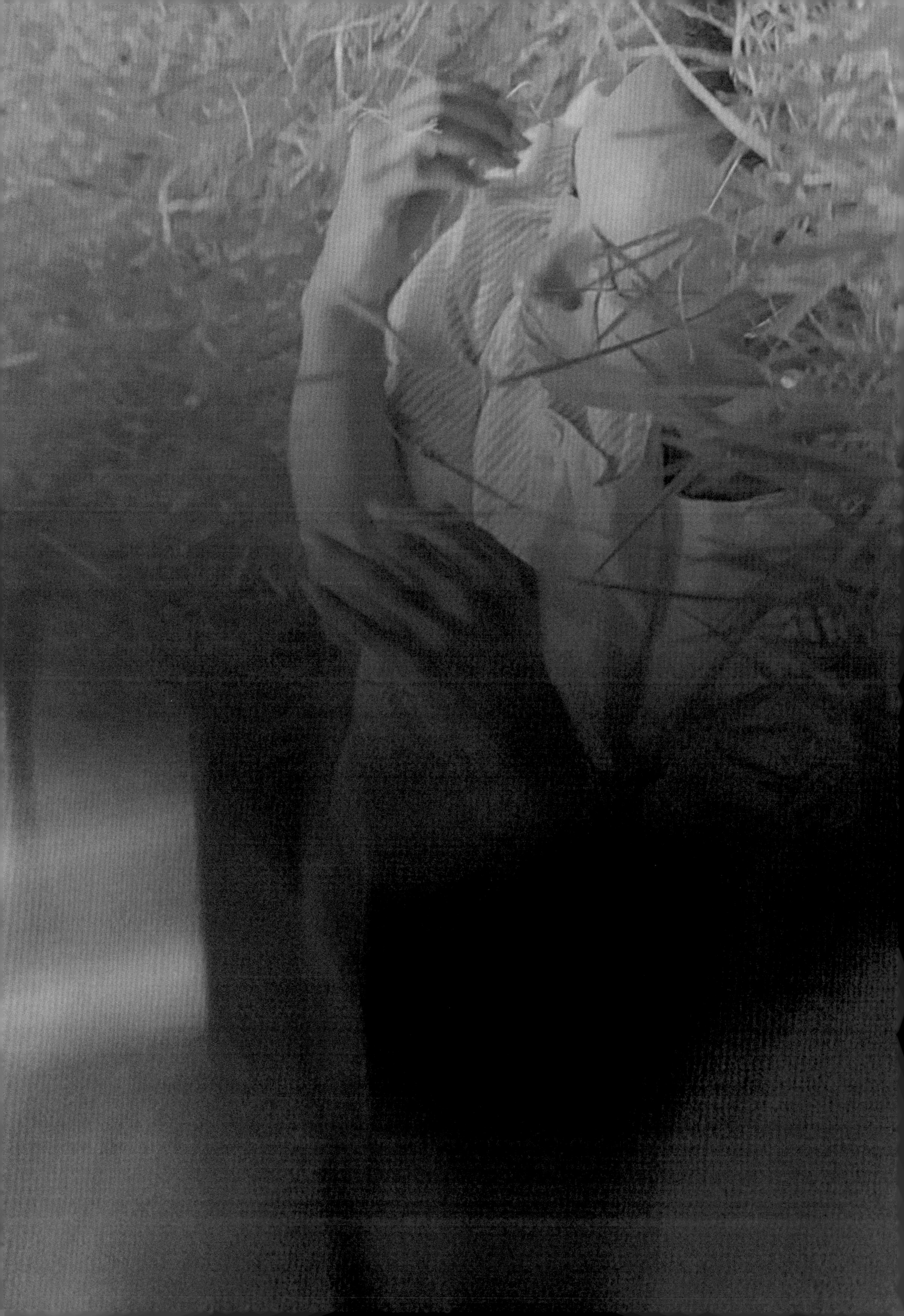

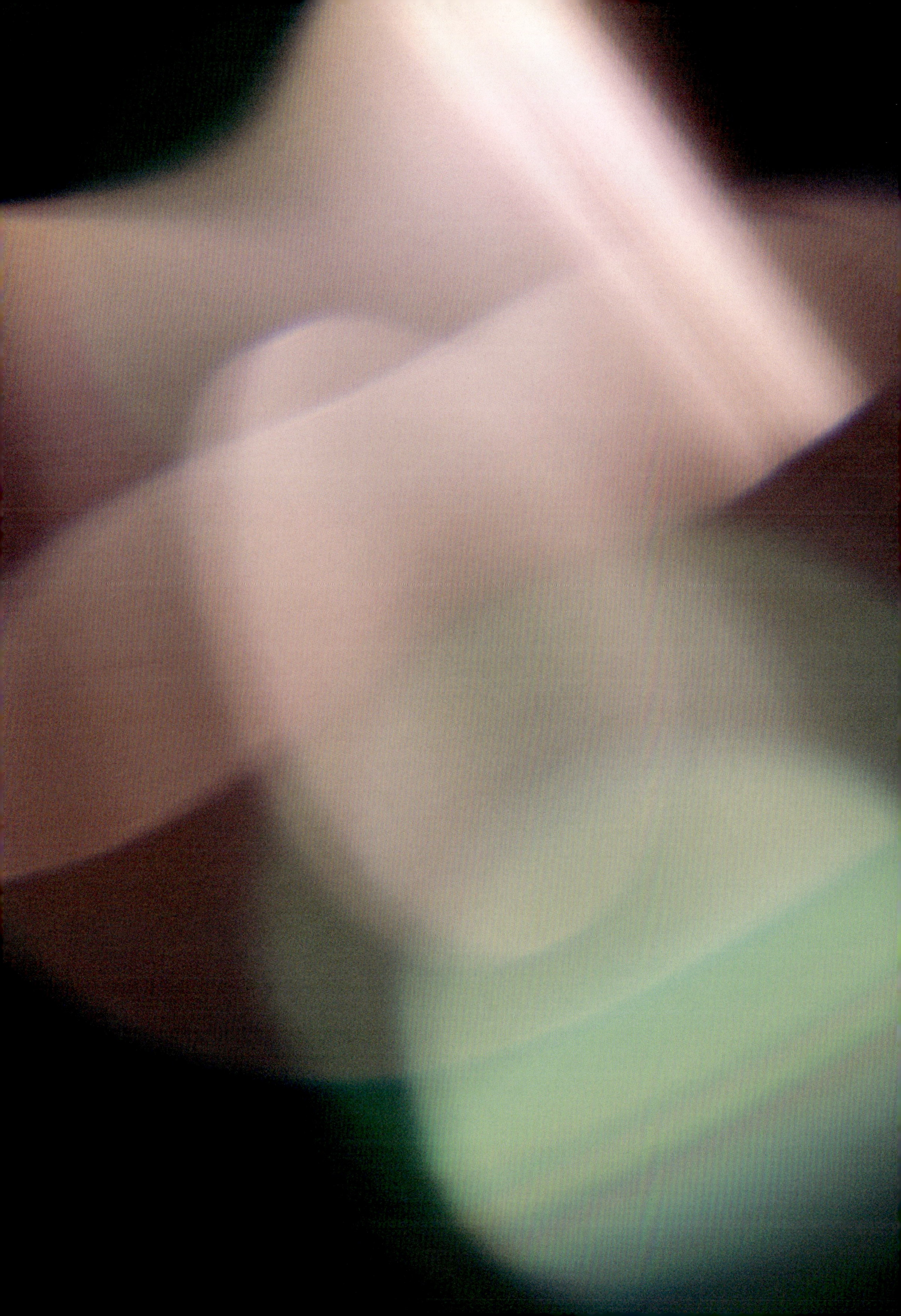

Trying
to hold it in

Like I said
piggy backing
on one

Garrett Bradley

Revolutions

Edited by Vincent van Velsen & Marente Bloemheuvel

Eye Filmmuseum

nai010 publishers

One More Time
(Running Around in Circles)
On Revolutions

Vincent van Velsen

'The word "revolution" was originally an astronomical term which gained increasing importance in the natural sciences through Copernicus' *De revolutionibus orbium colestium* (On the Revolutions of the Heavenly Spheres), 1543. In this scientific usage it retained its precise Latin meaning, designating the regular, lawfully revolving motion of the stars, which, since it was known to be beyond the influence of man and hence irresistible, was certainly characterised neither by newness nor by violence. On the contrary, the word clearly indicates a recurring, cyclical movement; (...) and was used metaphorically in the realm of politics. If used for the affairs of men on earth, it could only signify that the few known forms of government revolve among the mortals in eternal recurrence and with the same irresistible force which makes the stars follow their preordained paths in the skies. Nothing could be farther removed from the original meaning of the word "revolution" than the idea of which all revolutionary actors have been possessed and obsessed, namely, that they are agents in a process which spells the definite end of an old order and brings about the birth of a new world.' Hannah Arendt, *On Revolution*.

Revolutions

In 1572, scientists observed a previously unknown star, which remained visible for several years. In 1577, a comet passed close to Earth. Together, these celestial phenomena challenged the prevailing idea of a divinely created static universe. *On the Revolutions of the Heavenly Spheres*, which Copernicus published shortly before his death, in 1543, was thus supported and substantiated by observations. Expanding on earlier hypotheses and his predecessors' ideas, supplemented with new, extensive mathematical calculations, he described a simple model of our galaxy, with the Earth revolving around the Sun.

Unexpected Side Effects

In the 16th and 17th century, Revolution still meant 'restoration': a restoration of the political order. Like a planet in relation to the sun, a Revolution was a cyclical movement returning to a predetermined, previously visited point. Time moves on and we return to the same location or (political) situation. The term did not, therefore, refer to any innovative change, but to reverting to an earlier form (of government) or place. It wasn't until the 18th century that it became a political act aimed at restoration, one that unexpectedly sparked unforeseen consequences, setting in motion something beyond the realms of expectation which, rather than restoring the old order, led to the birth of something new.

'all stories begun and enacted by men unfold their true meaning only when they have come to their end...'

In the foreword to the Dutch edition of *On Revolution,* Ido de Haan writes that Hannah Arendt opposed 'deterministic or objectivist approaches to history in which revolutions are presented as explainable, inevitable, or even predictable historical events.' With which De Haan links Arendt's thinking to that of Walter Benjamin, who 'proposed

    One More Time (Running Around in Circles)

a fragmented historiography in which the past was preserved without assuming its historical necessity'. In other words, it was not about an 'accurate reproduction of the past, but of an image of the past shaped by imagination and judgement, in which new, unexpected, and unfulfilled possibilities of the past became visible.'

America God, America and God

The combination of Copernicus, Arendt, and Benjamin is fitting when thinking about Garrett Bradley. Her work *America* creates its own Revolution. Copernicus' radical, or revolutionary, idea that the Earth is not the centre of the universe, but part of a constellation of celestial bodies orbiting the Sun, is revolutionary to say the least. It was a radically new worldview, but also a world-changing concept when it comes to our place in the universe and in the world as we know it. If we then look at the images Garrett Bradley uses in *America* (2019), this is exactly what we see. Excerpts from the never-completed 1913 film *Lime Kiln Club Field Day* became part of *America*. Bradley supplemented parts of this production, starring Bert Williams, with contemporary footage that elaborates on forms of Black representation, individuals, and historic milestones. This is no 'accurate reproduction of the past'. Bradley uses fragments from history that actually existed but were unknown or forgotten – non-existent or presumed lost to history. These fragments are images of Black people, of a non-segregated movie production filmed during the early twentieth century. A film showing that Black people and white people joined hands and worked together. What we collectively remember from that time is segregation, violence, and negative stereotypes. And that memory is reinforced and, time after time, again and again, engrained in our collective visual conscience. Bradley shows that alternatives existed. That they still exist. That other ways of being together were – and still are – possible.

What do you imagine for your country?

We know the world, as Denise Ferreira da Silva says, in a way that ensures that we continue in our present systems. We think in the same cycles: 'thesis-antithesis-synthesis' (after Fichte). Criticism is part of our system; we do not change the deeper, underlying basis because centuries of thinking and doing have led us to this point. The deep-rooted perspectives, systems, and paradigms (according to Feyerabend) endure. We need to rid ourselves of them so we can interact with the world differently, *get to know the world differently.* On top of that, we tell each other – and share, pass on, and learn – all that knowing, in specific formats. And we shape the world and relate to nature, the universe, and one another on the basis of those stories, that knowledge. We may be thinking beings (Homo sapiens) but, above all, we are a storytelling species or, in the words of Sylvia Wynter, Homo narrans. We live a collective narrative.

Revolutions

A new insight, a new discovery, can change the entire narrative. It can be one small step for a person, but one giant leap for a country (America) or mankind. About where you stand as a person in the world; where you stand in relation to others, or where

Vincent van Velsen

we all stand in the universe. The discovery of the *Lime Kiln Club Field Day* fragments, combined with Bradley's reading, allows us to know history differently. It changes a self-image and a worldview. She tells a different story: a 'picture of the past shaped by imagination and judgement, in which new, unexpected, and unfulfilled possibilities of the past became visible.' Bradley creates Revolutions.

I imagine seeing myself

While Copernicus' celestial bodies revolve in all their grandeur, on Earth time passes with another revolution around the sun and its own axis. Days consist of hours, hours of minutes, minutes of seconds. Time moves on, and in the meantime, we live our lives and form relationships with others. It was from this micro focus that Langston Hughes and Roy DeCarava collaborated on *The Sweet Fly Paper of Life* (1955). At a time when perceptions of Black Americans were deeply negative and poverty was widespread, they wanted to tell a different story. But more than simply telling it, they wanted to show it. To capture everyday life. The intimacy, the joy, the togetherness, the love. Within a family, generations, and community. They got close and recorded, in words and images: Hughes and DeCarava presented an authentic story about an imaginary protagonist Mary Bradley (so, no relation to Garrett) and created a seminal work. Perception-changing; creating new collective knowledge by visualising a different narrative.

It starts from conversation

Such everydayness and intimacy rooted in reality is precisely what Garrett Bradley so adeptly captures. She gets close and stays there, often for a very long time. She builds rapport, follows people, travels with them, is present, supports and documents. Meanwhile, she makes a film. This is how she made *Time* (2020) and *Alone* (2017), *Osaka* (2021) and *Below Dreams* (2014). And in 2019, she made *AKA*. The focus is on relationships between Black women and women of colour: the relationship to their skin, to their kin, to how they perceive themselves, and each other. Hours of conversations formed the basis. The result was a relatively short, single channel work. Fragments from the interactions flit past, sporadically, but structurally. They offer hints and insights but never anything conclusive. They are snippets of knowledge that are passed on. The conversations helped to inform the images, but they are fragments, just as we always get to know people when they pass by, when we spend a little time with them: in part. We will never know the full story, but we certainly get a sense of the person. Film is redactive. It is made, framed, construed, incomplete. How do you transcend the incomplete image and move towards a whole idea? *AKA* creates it with feeling.

Are you colour struck?

In *a Negro, a Lim-o* (2022), Bradley moves closer towards abstraction without direct visualisation. She did this by entering into a direct interaction with the filmic material: we see the end result of her intervention within the camera; using her fingers she touched, manipulated, and tampered with the film, blurring and obscuring the recorded image. Yet it captures enough of what took place in front of the camera. It manages to convey the fragments, nonetheless. Moving shapes and silhouettes, no sharply detailed presences: a feeling materialises. An atmosphere is created.

I'd rather be with you

In collaboration with Arthur Jafa, Garrett Bradley made *a Negro, a Lim-o*, a video work that evokes the spirit of JAM – "Just Above Midtown was an art gallery and self-described laboratory led by Linda Goode Bryant that foregrounded African American artists and artists of colour. Open from 1974 until 1986, it was a place where Black art flourished and debate was cultivated". Drawing on each maker's personal relationship with the gallery, the people involved, and the interaction between the two artists, they created a work in which relationship is central. Two completely different people with two completely different (visual) languages side by side: one sometimes on the left, the other sometimes on the right, they both, and together, visually tell their story. One fast and bombastic, the other subtle and observant. Both coexistant. Not a linear narrative, but a conversation composed of fragments that convey an inner world.

Ultralight Beam (Father)

There is a moment in Arthur Jafa's *Love is the Message, the Message is Death* (2016) when scenes of the 1992 Olympic semi-final 400-metre sprint appear. Derek Redmond was the favourite but pulls his hamstring and collapses to the ground barely halfway through the race. His father rushes to him from the tribune. No one can stop Jim Redmond, and he reaches the track to help his son cross the finish line. For the race itself, the act had little meaning, but for the relationship and for the symbolic image, it was historic. The Black father who supports his son. After all the time already invested in getting to the Olympics Games. So many weekends on the track, so many mornings training, a competition every week, so many evenings leaving work early, making sure meals were eaten, making sure gear was ready and Derek was able to train. And now here, at this ultimate sports event, this ultimate moment, the body fails. And a second body is needed – again, here too – to support it. The Black father's love, care and support of his children is seldom portrayed. Films often show other, negative images, with cliches and stereotypes. The reality is rarely depicted, or the images that do exist are forgotten – and presumed lost to history.

Without love you're only an imitation

I cannot help but think that the urge for abstraction, the turn away from redactive representation, ties back to societal trends. In recent years, there was considerable interest in Black artists, particularly figurative painters like Amy Sherald, Henry Taylor, Lynette Yiadom Boakye, Jordan Casteel who all, in their own way, advocated Black representation. They portrayed Black people as dignified, and in their everydayness. This addressed, acknowledged, and, to some extent, compensated for historical underrepresentation and exclusion. Black people were welcome, were shown. This

Vincent van Velsen

wasn't just about the rich and famous people of colour as exceptional examples; everyday unknowns could also count on representation, because Black Lives Matter. But this is no longer a given. Society and politics took a turn, and Black people face renewed uncertainty about their lives and livelihoods. And in this current context, visibility also means being vulnerable.

Reality is an Excerpt on Television

Think of the covers of Beyoncé (Vogue, 2018) and Breonna Taylor (Vanity Fair, 2020), and the murals of George Floyd or the T-shirts with the face of Trayvon Martin. Think of the bodycam footage of the officer who shot dead Sonya Massey. We saw them, we said their names. But what has changed? How many were murdered? How many will follow? Despite the attention from politics and the arts, the stereotypes are unshakeable, the consequences are minimal. Everyday interactions are shaped by preconceived ideas of an other – someone we do not know and have never met, but have formed an image of, based on earlier images. The same is true of the biases embedded in the supposedly neutral systems that control us. Because BIPOC are more likely to be stopped and searched, and to be more harshly punished. Even if innocent. Wouldn't you then prefer to be completely invisible, unidentifiable and unclassifiable: to be abstract?

Politics? That's tricky

Abstraction is not only an art form, but also how systems and structures perpetuate their negative effects. And despite that fact that there was representation and accepted presence, the harmful structures are still very much present and in place. Because they are (red) lines extending from the past, through the present, and into the future. It is these partly invisible, partly unconscious, partly intangible structures that impact everyday lives of colour. What does it take to provide proof of an existence of a shared humanity or, as the French would say, a citizenship in unity, in equality, and in freedom? The turn away from visibility, and towards an inward focus, away from representation and embodiment, towards a more abstract presence, flourished among painters in the 1960s. Think of Jack Whitten, Sam Gilliam, Frank Bowling and Peter Bradley or more conceptual artists such as David Hammons and stanley brouwn. They used references to Black life and music, combined with materials and colours that hold specific meanings and resonances, alongside references to histories, geography or locations which, through abstraction, became symbols and shapes. They sought to create a feeling, and to portray and convey the African American experience.

Safe (I don't want to talk about it)

Where is the safe place in today's world? *AKA* focused on the skin, the interconnection with others, and the relationships between mothers and daughters. *Safe* (2022) contemplates the interior life. Here, too, Bradley explores the medium and the material. The images alternate, the continuous soundscape is the connecting factor within this poetic constellation. What does inner peace look like, the place of safety?

　　　　One More Time (Running Around in Circles)

Sheltered from the outside world, veiled in abstraction, Bradley posits the idea that this space is behind closed doors, behind one's closed eyelids. In this domain exists the radical political space of Black life. Indescribable but real. Impossible to capture on camera and thus based on abstraction and the creation of sphere. Evoking a feeling is where we have arrived.

Lasting Truth

The trilogy that *AKA* and *Safe* will form with a third work, yet to be created, is part of a circle. A revolution that takes us back to the experiments and attempts of our predecessors. Our parents and our intellectual peers, who faced similar questions in a different time. We know their worldviews, their experiences, their political metaphors, their stories and their knowledge, and we are also part of a movement that is irresistable and playing out beyond our influence. Unstoppable, but certainly not characterised by newness. The violence is ongoing, but we are moving towards what is preordained for us. Meanwhile searching for the right forms and appropriate places, for what we wish to convey. And if we think in revolutions, then the circle is complete: "All that you touch, You Change. All that you Change, Changes you. The only lasting truth Is Change."

This essay includes quotes from various works featured in the exhibition, alongside references to Hannah Arendt, Walter Benjamin, Octavia E. Butler, Mariah Carey, Daft Punk, Ido de Haan, Martin Luther King, Kanye West, Arthur Jafa, and the MoMA website about JAM.

          Vincent van Velsen

In Conversation:
Garrett Bradley & Rebecca Matalon

Rebecca Matalon: While we've worked together in the past, this is the first time we've sat down and recorded a conversation for publication, our first time 'on the record together'. Perhaps I should also acknowledge that we've known each other since our salad days, maybe something like 20 years at this point. I say this not to flex the fact that I've had the good fortune to have known you for so long, though that's certainly true, but to emphasise that I've also had the good fortune to watch your work grow and change over time.

We're here speaking today in relation to an exhibition at Eye Filmmuseum, *Garrett Bradley – Revolutions*, which is very much about time, cyclicality, change, as well as personal and political revolution. So the time span of our own lives together seemed important to state. But the notion of time also seemed like a good place to begin since it's both inherent to the medium of film as well as a subject of your work. I wonder if we might want to begin by talking about ideas of cyclicality, rotation, movement, and duration, and how you're currently thinking about these things. One way to do that, and we don't have to, but one way to do that would be to start with *America* (2019).

Garrett Bradley: Yeah it's a special thing to be able to talk with you over the course of these years. Time is changing. I mean, my relationship to time 20 years ago was so different, and I don't think just because of my age, but the world's relationship to time is really changing, (yet again), in a drastic way.

When Trump was elected for a second term last year, I was in Rome, and folks currently living in America were all talking through backup plans [laughing]. I'm not totally convinced that one exists. It might be that the only real option is to deal with and work through the place that one finds themself. Not only because fascism is rising almost everywhere (Italy included) but because truly, all we have is each other. The only way out is *through*.

When we talk about *cyclicality, rotation,* we're also referring to the way the world works. In nature, in ourselves and also collectively. It's the rotation that incites and supports revolution time and time again. We forget and then have to fight for what we remember (as a collective). Or the same problems in a new flavour appear and we remember we've been here before. That the commodification of our time, our attention, our right to autonomy are threatened generationally in new ways and so the revolution, again begins. I haven't addressed your question directly…

(R)(M): What you are saying about revolution and repetition is important. It reminded me that the origin of the word revolution, its Latin etymology, comes from the word *revolvere,* 'to roll back', and later, in the 15th century, it expands to mean recurrent changes. Although we now associate the word with a kind of forward motion, an idea of progress, I think it's important to hold onto this idea of revolution as a return, a repetition of ruptures. It makes me think of ebbs and flows. As you say, we've been here before.

Talking about being here before. This is the second time we've worked together on an exhibition. The first was in 2019 at the Contemporary Arts Museum, Houston, where I work, where we mounted your first solo museum exhibition

     In Conversation: Garrett Bradley & Rebecca Matalon

in the U.S., *Garrett Bradley: American Rhapsody.* It was also the first show I organised after relocating to Houston from Los Angeles. The show focused on three works, *America*, *Alone* (2017), and *AKA* (2019), two of which are included in the exhibition at Eye. I bring this up because despite the overlap in works, this show is very much intended to highlight different aspects of your practice. In *American Rhapsody* we really dug into the role that research plays in your work, specifically your engagement on the ground with communities and individuals whose stories you seek to tell, whether as the partner of someone who is navigating incarceration and the prison industrial complex, as women within interracial families, or with *America* your engagement with an archive, both existing and what Saidiya Hartman would call 'fabulated'. That earlier show really sought to introduce your practice as one dedicated to the specificity of Black life and Black lives through specific people, places, and histories. So it's interesting to hear you talk about this emphasis on collectivity right now. It feels like your practice at that moment was very grounded in a belief in the need to explore notions of America as an ideal, or a promise, or a concept through the individual stories of your subjects. Not to emphasise individualism over collectivity per se, but as a conceptual operating method that honours depictions of Black life that are specific and not universalising or all-encompassing.

In *America*, you're troubling linearity while working within a medium that demands it, right? You're thinking about the different ways that one can expand and contract time and history. Who gets to tell history and what does that telling look like? How do you rupture chronology and make it something that can be pulled apart and retold?

(G)(B): I think another way of putting it or part of the driving force for me is always to a certain extent around fairness. The work, I realise, is really always aiming in one way or another to rectify something that is untrue or not right in the world. Just as in my personal life, I work toward a bird dog point of a view: a multi-pronged perspective that maintains a sense of awareness on the ground, in a way that's intimate, personal and immediate without losing sight of how my choices are contributing to the bigger, collective picture. I approach my work the same way, and chronology is a big part of how I maintain that dual perspective.

'Black America', is America. And 'America' is a lie, a fantasy that evolved out of the churches in Europe to rationalise a desire for land, for expansion and domination, *by the word of God*. And then over here, in the States, that became *manifest destiny*. 'America' is Pol Pot's 'year zero'.[1] It's an erasure and denial of who and what was there before. A restart. So our very identity as 'Americans' is to say I am of 'zero'. I am of the *creation nation* of one-sided dreams. And Europe is not so different. They too have built and defined themselves on a fiction. The difference is that colonisation was executed elsewhere and so there is the illusion (I think) that one's culture is wholly their own, as opposed to also being an extraction and accumulation that encompasses many others.

So I was starting with what I knew, the place I knew the best and also a place I love and can't shake or leave behind, even when I want to. Because again,

1
'Year Zero' refers to the mandate enacted during Pol Pot's (1925 to 1997) time as the ruler of Cambodia from 1975–79. A leader of the totalitarian Khmer Rouge, Pot sought to 'reset the clock' by disposing of the country's history as well as its people to erase any and all traces of its past. During the reign of Pot and the Khmer Rouge regime, nearly two million Cambodians were killed.

    In Conversation: Garrett Bradley & Rebecca Matalon

where to…really? I'm from America, I call myself an American and I guess with the work, I felt like I needed to start there, with home. Where's the truth in my country, in me, in us? And *America* was made in New Orleans, which is not where I'm from, but where I now call home. I was born and raised in New York but have made a place here for the past 15 years because (and I wasn't totally conscious of it then when moving here in 2010) going back to chronology, I realised I had to go to the beginning which for me felt like the south. The genesis (and future) of the U.S.

(R)(M): As someone who is also currently living in the south, in what used to be Mexico, I hear what you're saying. The political context, the personal context of place matter. As does the acknowledgement that what we were sold as an 'American Dream', was always already a fantasy or a fiction. And I don't mean this exclusively in terms of upward mobility, home ownership, picket fences, and a couple of kids running in the yard, to quote The Beatles (another kind of British invasion!). I mean that the history we are taught about ourselves and our country–of course depending on who this 'self' is because maybe you're a self that doesn't even make it into the textbook–but the history we are taught is a fiction. The origin story of America as it has historically been told is that nothing was here, nothing existed in this place. Or if we are told the story, it's some version of cowboys and indians, and we all know what happens to the latter. But I wonder if what you're also really saying is that everything is a fiction? If you begin with or acknowledge that the idea of America is always a fiction, what does it mean to create new fictions as well, right? What does it mean to have the agency to build and shape new stories while understanding that history is always written by individuals with power. So what does it mean to contribute to that narrative and that telling as a kind of political act, as a way of working against erasure and as a way of telling a history, visualising a history that has been intentionally hidden or suppressed? I think it's interesting to think about the way that truth and fiction sort of intermingle in *America* to some extent.

(G)(B): I love this idea of *a new fiction*! But yeah…that makes me think of 2017-ish you know, when we saw confederate monuments across the country being removed. In New Orleans alone, I think there were about four in total.

There was (is) a debate happening around what to do with these objects that were representations of white supremacy in addition to the empty spaces that were made in their absence. When you remove history, you're also erasing it. And there is arguably something important about keeping those markers of our nation's history. So rather than removing, maybe adding-to? I don't want to look at General Lee when I'm driving downtown but I think forcing him to stay and witness us in tandem, be in conversation and truly contend with an equal presence would make me feel better and stronger than the illusion of resolve, when something is no longer visible.

(R)(M): When you erase history, you're more likely to repeat it.

(G)(B): Right. And that's humanity's Achilles heel, our propensity to forget. That's the rotation, the seed of constant revolution.

                  In Conversation: Garrett Bradley & Rebecca Matalon

(R)(M): But Lee was moved, right? I'm actually working with an artist named Mary Ellen Carroll right now that, back in 2013/14, proposed a project that would have involved putting rabbit ears on the Lee monument you speak of to transform it into an antenna, one that would provide wireless broadband to specific communities in the city that had consistently been denied access, or as they call it 'airlined' (essentially redlining but through airwaves). This was actually part of the same iteration of Prospect New Orleans that you were in. But I digress.

This question of what to do with these monuments is a potent one. There's actually an exhibition which has been in process for many years now and will finally open this fall at The Museum of Contemporary Art, Los Angeles, and The Brick (formerly LAXART) and organised by the artist Kara Walker with Hamza Walker and Bennett Simpson that will bring together decommissioned confederate statues and contemporary responses.

But just to go back, when you started making *America* it was during the Obama era, and I'm certainly not saying that I think Obama was a perfect president, but certainly there was a kind of optimism and openness that feels entirely absent in our present moment. Obviously not everywhere and not held by everyone, but it felt like there was a sort of reckoning with America's original sin, right? Maybe it was performative, but it felt like there was a much more public reckoning with histories of violence, enslavement, and racism that I can imagine buoyed this project along and really made it one of optimism as much as it was a corrective, as much as it was working to redress an absence of visual film depictions of everyday Black life and Black achievements. It was born from this moment or place of joy to some extent, right? I'm not saying your work has become pessimistic, but there's definitely something different happening in the works included in this exhibition. One is that your practice has moved increasingly towards abstraction, which is a sort of central argument of this specific exhibition.

But I wonder if there are ways in which this move towards abstraction feels like a necessary way of navigating how one images Blackness in our current climate or the climate of the last number of years, even before Trump's second term? In an earlier moment, when we were working on the show for CAMH, it felt like you had a commitment to a way of working that you believed might offer a way of refusing the tendency towards singular or totalising depictions of Blackness in favour of multiplicity. *Revolution* starts to pull at different threads. For me, it reflects turns or developments in your work, the seeds of which we can see, with hindsight, in *America* and *AKA,* particularly when placed in proximity to the two more recent works, *Safe* (2022) and *a Negro, a Lim-o* (2022). Those earlier works start to look more like portals or junctures, transitional works for lack of a better term. You seem less certain of visual cultures' emancipatory potential as a given.

(G)(B): Just a note on Obama. I think presidents matter. Figurehead or not, we are impressionable, we repeat what we see and hear and so the biggest voice will always have relevance, figurehead or not. The reason why there's never

     In Conversation: Garrett Bradley & Rebecca Matalon

been a perfect president is because 'a president' is an idea that was fabricated along with the 'dream' itself.

Legacy Russell's book, *Black Meme* (2024) makes a key observation on how violence against Black and Brown bodies, or our forced absences really, are in some cases the only presence that we have in visual culture. That this can be tracked prior to the internet but has taken on a whole new shape of course in the past 20 or so years alongside the internet. I titled the work, *America,* speaking in some ways to this very point, which was that everything eventually lands online and so how could the work (and us) disrupt the algorithm by offering more of a self-defined presence and more accurate, inclusive sense of American culture and history?

That was one way of thinking or working through the possibility of liberation, but I have to admit, that the goal of AI and the digitisation of the natural world being primarily a narrowing of reality and control of it, makes for real challenges when making things that will eventually get there. The work does, to a certain extent, start to bend and become beholden to the platform in which it's being seen. Alexandra Bell's work comes to mind in this as well. Her work is actively interrogating and holding responsible the manipulation of information and historical narrative within modern platforms like *the news* and in that way, is actively resisting and maintaining autonomy in ways others have a harder time doing.

You mentioned abstraction and the possibilities of it being inherently liberatory… it could be seen as a kind of armour, but I think I'd be robbing myself and those who came before me of a more accurate reasoning which is less about defense and more about the idea? The interest or question? And also — what's happening in its shape and form? This is what art is. And those questions have historically been reserved for mostly white male artists who are given the luxury of talking philosophy over their personal affiliations. But that doesn't mean when (we) start doing it, the rules need to change. Picasso found abstraction in Africa.

So I think maybe a shift toward a more abstract space is really about a new curiosity for me. *A camera is built to accurately capture.* The challenge or interest is how to get around that while still using these machines. In the same way I was thinking through a breaking of linearity in a very practical way with *America* – (literally how do you collapse and juxtapose time when you are limited by one frame at a time?) The question I'm interested in is how to do that with the camera itself, with the images it produces and can that *getting around* actually redefine our understanding of what is and isn't "accurate?"

Ⓡ Ⓜ: I don't think I said that abstraction was inherently liberatory. Or if I did, what I meant to suggest was the way it *might potentially* function as an exit strategy or an off ramp from the trap of representation in this moment – this isn't a new idea. (Cyclicality, again.) But I wonder if what you're speaking to is the camera as a tool of both transcription and mediation. How does one frustrate the camera as a mechanism – you're getting around. Which also brings up this idea of promiscuity, an impurity of form, a kind of corrupting of

In Conversation: Garrett Bradley & Rebecca Matalon

readability. I think this goes back to what you're saying about Russell's book and this question of a refusal of immediate legibility in an art world that demands that Black artists and artists of colour tell certain narratives through certain mediums, namely through figuration and depictions of the body. And within this paradigm that the body and identity are synonymous, and that identity is singular. We would do well to hold on to Fred Moten's call for opacity. Or Édouard Glissant's identification of departure (a kind of getting around) "as the moment one consents not to be a single being."[2] Of course, Glissant is speaking of departure as diaspora.

Your point about the permission granted to white male artists, the ways in which questions of form and materiality, the philosophical properties of one's practice are taken as a given when whiteness is involved, are important. When whiteness is the default (and it too often is), there is a tendency to use identity and race as a primary lens in critically analysing or interpreting a work that depicts a non-white body. This essentialising is problematic. How do you evade or move away from that sort of trap, that double bind? To some extent I suppose I'm talking about reception versus production, but I think we all know that once a work leaves a studio and circulates (online, in museums, anywhere really) it becomes open to interpretation, welcome or not.

Some of the things you're saying come up in the conversation that you had with Linda Goode Bryant and Arthur Jafa published in *Devotion* (2024). That conversation happened in relation to the collaborative work you made with Jafa, *a Negro, a Lim-o* (2022), which was commissioned on occasion of the exhibition *Just Above Midtown: Changing Spaces* (2022). That show honoured the groundbreaking work of Bryant who founded the New York gallery, Just Above Midtown (JAM), in 1974 as a site dedicated to experimental and radical work by Black artists and artists of colour.

It's interesting to talk about violence and the trap of representation in relation to *a Negro, a Lim-o* or more precisely in relation to you and Jafa as artmakers who often use film or video. I don't know if you mind if I jump over there, but there's something I started to realise, which is that Jafa's work tends to be quite violent. He tends to use found footage of brutal violence enacted upon Black bodies in his work, alongside the more ecstatic and celebratory depictions of achievement. There is a way, in the conversation between the three of you, that you get a sense of the ways he comes from a place of pessimism to some extent. I don't mean that as a condemnation, but generally, his videos are ecstatic, but they're tinged with violence, both real and latent. This violence has a name and its name is whiteness. His works can be brutal to watch and intentionally so. But there's something about *a Negro, a Lim-o* where it feels like Jafa is maybe careening towards Black joy. I mean, the video ends with a baby being born!

Your work, on the other hand, tends to operate from a place of optimism, I think. But there's something about your contribution to that collaborative work, which features ripples and ruptures and distortions, that feels like it's coming from a darker place. It's interesting to me to experience that work, to some extent, as a role reversal. Maybe that's completely untrue. But you expect

2   Manthia Diawara, *Conversation with Édouard Glissant Aboard the Queen Mary II*, August 2009. Translated by Christopher Winks. Last accessed April 21, 2025. https://www.liverpool.ac.uk/media/livacuk/csis-2/blackatlantic/research/Diawara_text_defined.pdf

Jafa's work to be brutal, to employ disquieting and devastating imagery. The footage you shot for that work, which includes abstracted scenes from New Orleans but also a road in Raceland, Louisiana, holds the history of these sites including histories of enslavement, violent massacres of Black residents, but also in our contemporary times, sites known for prisons and the petrochemical industry. So we're talking about the long arm of slavery and racism, including environmental racism.

(G)(B): The jumping off point, the question that we started with in talking through that collaboration was, 'what is Black art?'. That was the question Bryant was interrogating (both directly and indirectly) with JAM as a collective space. And our work together, it was also being reframed in relation to the show at MoMA.

For Jafa and I, it was really about, do we want to answer that question? And then I think we decided like – no, forget – the question. The question is the problem, you know what I mean? But then I think we did answer the question [laughing] by sort of allowing it to metabolise in ourselves the way that we creatively felt most compelled to do. Which was to just do our thing. It was beautiful that Bryant brought us together because, you know, my feeling is that in an outward-facing way, our work probably appears really different. But I think actually the intentionality behind what we do, our focus and obsession, is similar, you know? Jafa's work is equally as optimistic. And what we did, might really be about how violence and beauty can work together to the same end, you know? We intertwined by being ourselves.

Going back to this thing around mitigation and the obscuring of the image and of abstraction and the role of bodies. I mean, I was really focused on how I might think through subject matter and form in a way that's less separate, in a way that's a little bit more blurry, literally, as I mentioned a bit earlier. The final piece also came out of that effort and interest.

(R)(M): It's interesting because certainly this question of what is Black art may have been the impetus for the work, right? That was the prompt for it. But it's interesting, at least for me, that what you actually made opens up new and different questions, and part of that just comes from the fact that you're juxtaposing two different artists' responses, you know, that you're trying to cohere two different imagistic regimes at one moment, right? It's a two-channel video, you see both of the channels in front of you, the channels flip at times. While this question of what is Black art may have been a framework, something else happens in its making, to some extent, right? It feels like this dual vision of what it might mean to image a past and present history in different ways. Yes, you both might be thinking through and exploring similar ideas, but in the end, visually, your work is different. The sort of way you tell the stories, the way you render that history is radically different, at least for me.

(G)(B): I think also what I'm hearing maybe is that the double vision of it takes on its own vision, like its own thing, which is really the genius of Bryant. She gave us the challenge of making something together that is both about our own practices and also about the bigger picture at the same time. *The bird dog view* (laughing).

     In Conversation: Garrett Bradley & Rebecca Matalon

(R)(M): It feels like a really beautiful synergy of each of your working methods, even if it seems like, as I proposed at the beginning, each of you is departing from, or seeming to depart from, comfort zones. I keep coming back to juxtaposition, the idea that when you place one thing next to another, they change, right? They don't stay the same. Something else happens. And you're creating a third thing.

(G)(B): Exactly. I think it's also important to mention that part of what JAM as a space was able to facilitate and foster was disagreement and fierce debate and a collective conversation around these big questions around what art was and what Black art was, as well as what it wasn't. I think that's really shifted today. The art of disagreement has really been threatened, you know? We've lost sight of the fact that what we believe is not who we are.

When someone disagrees with you, they're not disagreeing with who you are fundamentally as a human being, right? If we take away our religion, our politics, our identities even. We're still *someone*. Who is that?

(R)(M): I mean, that feels like it all goes back to a sort of rampant individualism, right? The total breakdown of any kind of social contract that might exist or once existed. Certainly, being in Texas, this feels to be true in the ways it feels like many people value self above all else. I mean, we're referred to as The Lone Star State, which says it all. So, of course, if we're seeing self-interest above all else, every disagreement or conflict is going to be seen as a direct attack on individual liberty.

To your point, yes, I actually think that conflict can be productive. I don't know… I don't know if we're in a moment that can ever be repaired. Maybe I'm thinking more negatively, but certainly there's been a kind of rupture, right? The belief in our collective responsibility, our responsibility to care for each other, is gone. I think part of that comes from a notion of self-protection as well as the false idea that other people's freedom and other people's success come at the cost of your own… The 'Don't Tread on Me', mentality for lack of a better term. But, you know, it's also nothing new. It's part of the long arc of neoliberalism and the even longer arc of capitalism.

(G)(B): I'd say dogma really, a fix-ed-ness which we find across the board. When we think about bringing two artists together from different generations with different ways of getting to the same question, what happens? Are we able to do that? You know, so I think that was also the other part of what was really interesting about working together. In this moment where we have really lost a lot of our tools for being able to coexist through difference, how do we do that together? It felt like a sport kind of, and it was fun – that's what it should be, you're pushing one another. It was the differences that unified us and in which our foundational similarities, I think, could even be highlighted.

(R)(M): It's like a double simultaneous vision, which, you know, feels very true to what that project was, the sort of, again, multiplicity of positions contained there. But, you know, one thing I also want to talk about in this same capacity as

    In Conversation: Garrett Bradley & Rebecca Matalon

your work is shifting towards abstraction, there's this coincident move towards an exploration of installation and how you present a film. You start to move away from a single channel projection onto a wall and towards thinking about the spatial components of film and video, right? How do you shift from that flatness to a kind of sculptural quality, which I think you've been doing, at least as we see in *America* and in *Safe*, which is the second chapter in a trilogy that also includes *AKA*. I'm interested if you could talk about that sort of evolution of your work as well, *America* as a juncture into the three-dimensional space of installation.

Ⓖ Ⓑ: It wasn't totally arbitrary, and it wasn't about trying to get outside of the theatrical experience. *America* specifically, was again, really about starting with the ideas. And the idea was to look at chronology and how, if we can understand the (real) order of something and make those transparent, does it give us a better understanding of our present moment? It felt to me that there was a very natural way in which that question could be physically articulated. So the reason that we're looking at four translucent flags in the form of an X in the 360-degree cycle, (the intersection), is to encourage viewers to make connections for themselves based on their own curiosity and agency to move through space. The work is proposing multiple perspectives, and the viewer is also contributing their own. It's a metaphor maybe for how history works. The physicality of the work was a necessary way of expressing and exploring a non-linear question.

The guiding principles that informed *Safe* were much more private, internal and sonically motivated. It was in many ways riffing off Kevin Quashie's proposal that the interior of ourselves, although elusive in nature, exists in parallel to the outside world and is equally as radical, even political, despite being dismissed as a result of its intangibility. When I started meditating, I could see my thoughts rather than being them. I could observe them from a distance, and I was able to understand more clearly how my sonic environment was not only in conversation but shaping the way in which I felt and saw the world. Or... how the same rotating thoughts could shift in tone, depending on the sounds around me. The work is made up of three channels, each channel in a different area of the space. And it's the same image, (the same thought), on rotation. What changes is the universal sound across all three. So again, a kind of hyper literal transference that informed the physicality and the way in which we move create meaning around and with the work.

Ⓡ Ⓜ: To go back to *America*, I want to say that it feels incredibly important to mention the way that, as a result of its spatial configuration and the translucent fabric you use for the screens, it becomes impossible to see a single image or sequence. You are always looking through one onto another. The screen becomes a lens. Which I think is not coincidental and an incredibly poetic and powerful gesture.

But in terms of rotation as image, it's a visual analogy that also extends to viewership, though, right? Both works depict scenes in which movement, spinning, rotating, become potent metaphors. But the works also demand that the viewer ambulate in a similar manner. So to fully see *America,* we as viewers

    In Conversation: Garrett Bradley & Rebecca Matalon

have to move around the installation in a way that mirrors the movement of the action of the film. Whether that's Bert Williams and Odessa Warren Gray on a carousel, whether that's the scene of disco balls rotating, whether that's the scene of lovers embracing, you know, there's this reciprocity between the sort of rotational movement depicted and the demand that as a viewer you orient yourself in relationship to this rotational moment, that your physical experience is one of moving around the work.

I think to some extent that's happening as well with *Safe*. There's this sort of negotiation between the movement on screen, the sort of conceptual ideas of movement and revolution and revolving, but then there's also the sort of phenomenological experience.

> (G)(B): Exactly. The physical nature is always (must even, speaking of dogma), I think be connected to an idea. What results from taking a concept or inquiry seriously and pursuing it to some end, is I think, what motivates the end result, the final thing we see.

(R)(M): Yeah, what's the conceptual underpinning? To some extent we're also talking about tempo – both the tempo of the sequence of images in a film and the tempo of the body moving through space. With *America* this tempo shifts throughout the film, it sort of dilates. *Safe* is decisively slower, as is your contribution to *a Negro, a Lim-o*. Time slows down. This makes me think about past conversations we've had about the ways in which social media and the internet have changed the culture of how we receive images. How images circulate. Certainly it seems to be an area that fascinates you and that you're thinking about a lot. But I'd also say that, to my mind, that sort of rapid speed in which we see images circulate is something that hasn't necessarily impacted your practice materially. I don't mean that it hasn't impacted your thinking but that your work and the way you work and the way your films and videos take shape, there's an emphasis on a kind of radical slowness, right? That's really compelling and blatantly antagonistic to the ways we currently tend to experience images, whether it's on TikTok or Instagram or some other kind of social media platform. I think that's also one of the things I really loved about the productive juxtaposition that happens in *a Negro, a Lim-o* between your work and Jafa's. But, you know, to keep moving forward, there's something to be said about that slowness as a sort of radical practice in and of itself in the way that it demands slow looking and attention from a viewer, right? It demands a different kind of tempo from a viewer.

> (G)(B): Yeah, I mean, going back to the beginning of our conversation, I think what's unprecedented about this moment is the quality of and way in which we are experiencing the speed of things. And I think it's a natural instinct to try to define what's happening in real time as a way of feeling in control, feeling safe. That definition is comforting...but my speed, someone else's speed... the impulses that arrive in this landscape for each of us, it's maybe the same conversation of *violence or joy, attack, or respite*...they all work hand in hand. The beauty of art is that everyone gets to (and should), do it their own way and then it all comes together to create a conversation, and true vision of time. We exist in a collection of perspectives, and it all adds up to (a) bigger picture.

　　　　In Conversation: Garrett Bradley & Rebecca Matalon

(R)(M): Maybe what you're getting at is the way that slowness matters and means something *in relation* to quickness or the rapid speed, right? It gains meaning in juxtaposition, dialectically, as a different way of working.

I thought that we could end with the elephant in the room, which is the current film you're working on, which is an adaptation of Octavia E. Butler's prophetic 1993 science fiction novel, *Parable of the Sower*. We don't have to go into details about the production. I know it's very hush-hush. But the project is also very much about cyclicality and change, to sort of bring us back to where we started. To quote some of the central tenets of the story's main character, Lauren Oya Olamina, "All that you touch You Change. All that you Change Changes you. The only lasting truth Is Change." I guess the one question I have is if working on this project, *Parable of the Sower,* which you've been doing for some time, if it has impacted your work more broadly?

(G)(B): Lauren's story requires a certain kind of distance we don't have any more, which is a challenge. Maybe *the* challenge. And so I think one way to ensure it remains useful is to mine the proposed solution within her experience and make it clear and tangible.

How the project has impacted my work, I guess, is to be seen, but what the process has emphasised and clarified for me is the importance of an ongoing pursuit in to believe in the possibility of true societal. A future which relies on remembrance and the full circle from which we started.

    In Conversation: Garrett Bradley & Rebecca Matalon

America

2019

**Multi-channel video installation;
35mm film transferred to HD video
(black-and-white, sound);
23:55 minutes
Courtesy the artist and Lisson Gallery**

Marked by a kind of propulsive force, *America* (2019) reconstructs an absent visual record of Black life in early 20th century America through a series of 12 black-and-white vignettes coupled with found footage from what is believed to be the earliest surviving film to feature a Black cast and integrated production crew. While Bradley moves sequentially through time, reinterpreting specific historical or cultural events between 1915 and 1926, these scenes are ruptured by archival footage from *Lime Kiln Club Field Day* (1913). In *America*, Bradley refuses a traditional linear narrative structure by employing multiple channels and asynchronous imagery. Projected across four hanging, translucent fabric screens arranged to form a broken X, the artist's imagery overlaps. Each projection surface is both a screen and a lens through which we see not only the images before us but those unfolding on surrounding screens. Further, the broken X configuration encourages (if not requires) viewers to move around and between the screens, our movement around the form echoing the film's emphasis on rotational movement in scenes that include a merry-go-round, spinning disco balls, and a revolving door, to name just a few.

America's soundtrack is rhythmic and rhapsodic. In addition to the prominent use of Foley, Bradley worked with composer Trevor Mathison (of the Black Audio Film Collective) to create an ambient score that takes us in and out of time and place. Scenes that would seem to situate us in the early 20th century are coupled with the wail of a police siren that is distinctively, perhaps even menacingly, contemporary or the deep drawl of a man repeating the word 'America'. *America* refutes any idea of history and its telling as a purely intellectual exercise, emphasising instead the bodily and experiential aspects of knowledge where visual and sonic perception are crucial forms of knowing. The earliest work by Bradley included in this publication, as well as her first foray into installation, *America* reflects a way of working that remains both urgent and essential to the artist's practice, one that privileges the fragmentary, stuttering effects of dissonance over narrative cohesion.

AKA

2019

Single channel HD video
(colour, sound);
8:17 minutes
Courtesy the artist and Lisson Gallery

If *America* and other early films by Bradley tend to draw attention to the often slow, unremarkable unfolding of daily life in the US, specifically Black life, with *AKA* (2019) the artist moves increasingly towards the hallucinatory and prismatic. The work is the first in an ongoing trilogy of films that also includes *Safe* (2022), shown in this publication. Like many of Bradley's films, the experimental short developed out of hours-long conversations, in this instance between the artist and Black mothers and daughters born into mixed-race families or families of the same race with varying skin tones. She began with a series of questions regarding race, upward mobility, and the relationship between white women and Black women, which the artist posed to friends and family, and on social media. In one instance, one of Bradley's subjects repeatedly asked her mother, "Are you colour struck?" The term, made famous by Zora Neale Hurston's 1925 play of the same name, refers to the notion of 'colourism', which describes both interracial and intraracial forms of discrimination based on the colour of one's skin. Bradley subsequently used the phrase to shape the visual and sonic landscape of the film – specifically *AKA*'s shimmering effects, which contribute to the film's dream-like atmosphere. Shots of clouds in the sky and prismatic colour fields merge with images of the women in cars, looking through family photos, tending to a garden, and reflected in rippling water. Bradley intersperses audio recordings of her subjects riffing on colourism with sounds of dripping water, whooshing wind, crashing waves, a heartbeat, birds, and other ambient sounds. In works like *AKA* and its sister film, *Safe*, Bradley emphasises an idea of revolution that is always equally celestial and earthly, personal and communal.

a Negro, a Lim-o

2022

**Two-channel video
(colour, sound);
27:31 minutes
Courtesy the artists, Lisson Gallery,
Gladstone Gallery, and Sprüth Magers**

Originally commissioned by The Museum of Modern Art in New York as part of the exhibition *Just Above Midtown: Changing Spaces* (2022), *a Negro, a Lim-o* (2022) is a collaboration between Bradley and artist Arthur Jafa. The exhibition honoured the groundbreaking work of Linda Goode Bryant who founded the New York gallery, Just Above Midtown (JAM), in 1974 as a site dedicated to experimental and radical work by Black artists and artists of colour. While committed to giving a platform to Black artists, JAM crucially sought to trouble any singular definition of Black art.

The two-channel projection opens with Jafa's archival footage of a live performance by legendary funk musician Bootsy Collins and Bootsy's Rubber Band juxtaposed with Bradley's blur of black-and-white imagery featuring pulsating and rippling glitch-like effects. Her abstract forms appear almost ethereal, hovering over a series of scenes barely legible as a country road or bodies in motion. Almost halfway through the work, the channels flip (and continue to do so throughout), funk turns to a more solemn musical piece on piano and horn, which is further overlayed by the crackling static of a record player. Bradley's slowly unfolding and ghostly scenes take a different tempo than Jafa's, whose signature found imagery culled from the internet and social media sites tends to shift rapidly across the screen. In the end, a baby is born. Fade to black.

If Jafa's sources tend to announce themselves, Bradley's are more cryptic and intentionally so. While her footage may appear to be digitally manipulated, the distortions we see in Bradley's contribution were made in-camera. Although abstract, the scenes remain haunted by the histories of the places depicted – her hometown of New Orleans, but also Raceland, Louisiana in Lafourche Parish, a former home to sugar cane plantations and the site of a violent massacre of Black residents in 1887 at the hands of an all-white militia, and, more recently, grounds of a $40 million dollar penitentiary. In *a Negro, a Lim-o*, we see the artist use abstraction to smuggle in a history of ongoing violence, dispossession, and tyranny, while using formal experimentation to emphasise moving images' capacity to foreground feeling over knowing.

Safe

2022

**Three-channel HD video
(colour, black-and-white, sound);
continuous duration
Courtesy the artist and Lisson Gallery**

The second film in Bradley's ongoing trilogy, *Safe* (2022) uses strategies of juxtaposition, repetition, and doubling. If *AKA* meditates on the ways in which visual culture – including American cinema – has shaped intergenerational relationships between Black women, *Safe* focuses on interiority and the impossibility of ever fully representing the psychic life of a subject.

The film's three channels are linked by a single soundtrack that includes birds, the hum of cicadas, a crackling fire, alongside police sirens, car horns, and the whir of a helicopter. Bradley's use of rippling and shimmering effects, as well as mirroring, become visual metaphors for the refusal of a cohesive or singular self. On one channel of the work a woman rolls slowly down a hillside with her eyes closed, her rotating body signalling both the freeness of youthful abandon and the ways in which revolution is always in part an embodied act. On the left side of the screen, blackness is broken up by glistening halos of red and green light that, at times, encroach upon the woman's body. This same woman – the dancer and choreographer Donna Crump with whom Bradley has previously collaborated – appears across all three channels, coming in and out of focus, in fragments, doubled, or distorted. *Safe* offers abstraction as both a political position and a form of resistance, one that proposes an alternative to the circumscribed ways in which Blackness and Black womanhood are depicted and delimited in visual culture.

Garrett Bradley – Revolutions

Garrett Bradley (b. 1986) explores how historical images shape our view of the world. Her work – encompassing narrative, documentary and experimental film – shows an increasing tendency towards abstraction and the sculptural. Bradley invites us to take a step back and reflect on the question: What are we actually looking at? In doing so, she makes the viewer aware of the pitfalls of representation and unravels the mechanisms that determine how we perceive ourselves and others.

This publication accompanies the exhibition *Revolutions*, presented at Eye Filmmuseum from 14 June to 7 September 2025. The exhibition was initiated following Garrett Bradley's receipt of the Eye Art & Film Prize in 2023, an award that recognizes artists whose work makes a significant contribution at the intersection of film and visual art.

Both the exhibition and this accompanying publication take their title, *Revolutions*, from the various forms of revolution found in Garrett Bradley's work. A revolution can mean a political shift in power, but also a cycle – like the rotation of the earth on its axis, marking the passage of time. Bradley's work reveals the revolutionary potential of the everyday: the change sparked by small acts of resistance.

Bregtje van der Haak, director of Eye Filmmuseum: "Garrett Bradley creates bold and visually compelling work that tackles themes such as racism and exclusion with exceptional energy, expressed through a mix of media, including archival footage. Her (documentary) films and installations reference, among other things, the struggle for social justice and the political history of the United States, while exploring deeply human emotions such as anger and sorrow."

Eye Art & Film Prize

In 2023 Garrett Bradley won the Eye Art & Film Prize, awarded annually to an artist or filmmaker who has made an important contribution at the intersection of film and visual art. Each year an international jury and advisory board, consisting of key players from the world of (visual) art and film, selects the winner. Other winners were Hito Steyerl (2015), Ben Rivers (2016), Wang Bing (2017), Francis Alÿs (2018), Meriem Bennani (2019), Kahlil Joseph (2020), Karrabing Film Collective (2021), Saodat Ismailova (2022), Chia-Wei Hsu (2024) and Sohrab Hura (2025).

Jury 2023

Chris Dercon (BE/FR)
managing director of the Fondation Cartier pour l'art contemporain, Paris

Nanouk Leopold (NL)
filmmaker, theatre director, visual artist

Nalini Malani (IN)
visual artist

Lemohang Jeremiah Mosese (LS/DE)
filmmaker and visual artist

Hila Peleg (IL/DE)
curator and filmmaker

Bregtje van der Haak
chair, director of Eye Filmmuseum

International Advisory Board 2023

Farah Clémentine Dramani-Issifou (BJ/FR)
curator, film programmer, researcher and critic

Solange Farkas (BR)
director and curator of Associação Cultural Videobrasil

Andrea Lissoni (IT/DE)
artistic director of Haus der Kunst, Munich

Cuauhtémoc Medina (MX)
curator, critic, art historian

Hoor Al Qasimi (AE)
president and director of the Sharjah Art Foundation

Rajendra Roy (US)
head curator Film at MoMA, New York

Eva Sangiorgi (IT/AT)
artistic director of VIENNALE, Vienna International Film Festival

Apichatpong Weerasethakul (TH)
filmmaker

Jaap Guldemond
chair, Eye Filmmuseum

The Eye Art & Film Prize is supported by Ammodo.

This publication coincides with the exhibition
Garrett Bradley – Revolutions
Eye Filmmuseum, Amsterdam
14 June – 7 September 2025

Eye Filmmuseum
IJpromenade 1
1031 KT Amsterdam
The Netherlands
info@eyefilm.nl

EXHIBITION

The exhibition *Garrett Bradley – Revolutions* is organised
by Eye Filmmuseum in close collaboration with Rebecca
Matalon, Senior Curator, Contemporary Arts Museum
Houston

Director Eye:
Bregtje van der Haak
Head of Exhibitions:
Vincent van Velsen
Coordinator Exhibitions:
Marente Bloemheuvel
Project Managers:
Reinier Klok, Julia Kozakiewicz
Production Assistant:
Sebastián Vásquez
Exhibition Texts:
Rebecca Matalon, Vincent van Velsen
Graphic Design:
Joseph Plateau, Amsterdam
Translation:
Billy Nolan
Film programmer:
Thijs Havens
Publicity and Marketing:
Lisette Ruijtenberg, Aubéry Escande, Rachel Voorbij
Eye Art & Film Prize Coordinator:
Judith Öfner
Development & Sponsoring:
Susan Gloudemans, Leontien Boogaard, Annelien Winters
Technical Production:
Rembrandt Boswijk, Indyvideo, Utrecht and Martijn Bor
Audiovisual Equipment:
MHB, Joure; Redbox, Utrecht
Installation:
Syb Sybesma, Surinamekade.nl, Amsterdam
Lighting:
Maarten Warmerdam, Studio Warmerdam, Amsterdam
Lettering:
Riwi ColloType, Amsterdam

PUBLICATION

Edited by:
Vincent van Velsen and Marente Bloemheuvel
Texts:
Garrett Bradley, Rebecca Matalon, Vincent van Velsen
Texts on works:
Rebecca Matalon
Graphic Design:
Bardhi Haliti, Amsterdam
Translation and copy-editing:
Lisa Holden
Project Manager:
Laurence Ostyn, naio10 publishers Rotterdam
Lithography:
Marc Gijzen
Printing:
Wilco, Amersfoort
Publisher:
Eye Filmmuseum, Amsterdam &
naio10 publishers Rotterdam

Acknowledgements:
Garrett Bradley
Rebecca Matalon
Chris Fedorak
Lisson Gallery, London, New York, Los Angeles, Shanghai,
Beijing
Gladstone Gallery, New York, Los Angeles, Brussels, Seoul
Sprüth Magers, Berlin, London, Los Angeles, New York
Members of the Jury and Advisory Board of the Eye Art &
Film Prize
Ammodo for their support of the Eye Art & Film Prize

© 2025, the artist, authors, photographers,
Eye Filmmuseum Amsterdam and naio10 publishers
Rotterdam

naio10 publishers is an internationally orientated publisher
specialized in developing, producing and distributing books
in the fields of architecture, urbanism, art and design.
www.naio10.com

naio10 books are available internationally at selected
bookstores and from the following distribution partners:
North, Central and South America – Artbook | D.A.P.,
New York, USA, dap@dapinc.com
Rest of the world – Idea Books, Amsterdam,
the Netherlands, idea@ideabooks.nl

For general questions, please contact naio10 publishers
directly at sales@naio10.com or visit our website
www.naio10.com for further information.

Printed and bound in the Netherlands

ISBN   978-94-6208-932-7
BISAC   ART060000, PER004040
NUR   640, 740

The exhibition is made possible by:
LISSON GALLERY

Main Partner Eye:
VRIENDENLOTERIJ